Library and Archives Canada Cataloguing in Publication

MacLeod, Elizabeth, author
How to become an accidental genius / Elizabeth MacLeod & Frieda Wishinsky;
illustrated by Jenn Playford.

Includes bibliographical references and index.
Issued in print and electronic formats.
ISBN 978-1-4598-1676-3 (hardcover).—ISBN 978-1-4598-1677-0 (PDF).—
ISBN 978-1-4598-1678-7 (EPUB)

1. Inventors—Biography—Juvenile literature. 2. Inventors—
Juvenile literature. 3. Inventions—History—Juvenile literature.
4. Inventions—Juvenile literature. 5. Serendipity in science—Juvenile
literature. I. Wishinsky, Frieda, author II. Playford, Jennifer, illustrator
III. Title.

T39.M33 2019   j609.2'2   C2018-904708-9
                      C2018-904709-7

Simultaneously published in Canada and the United States in 2019
Library of Congress Control Number: 2018954163

Summary: This nonfiction book for middle readers is full of inspiring tales of inventors and innovators who have accidentally changed the world. The book also features profiles of inventive kids and teenagers.

Orca Book Publishers is dedicated to preserving the environment and has printed this book on Forest Stewardship Council® certified paper.

Orca Book Publishers gratefully acknowledges the support for its publishing programs provided by the following agencies: the Government of Canada, the Canada Council for the Arts and the Province of British Columbia through the BC Arts Council and the Book Publishing Tax Credit.

Illustrations by Jenn Playford

Edited by Sarah N. Harvey
Design by Teresa Bubela
Cover illustration by Jenn Playford

ORCA BOOK PUBLISHERS
orcabook.com

Printed and bound in China.

22 21 20 19 • 4 3 2 1

CONTENTS

INTRODUCTION

How do you become an accidental genius?

And how does an accident lead to innovation, invention or a scientific breakthrough?

One thing's for sure. Most innovation doesn't happen overnight. Most innovators think about a problem for a long time before attempting a solution. Most experience failure before success.

And what about "genius"?

"Genius" is seeing failures and accidents as opportunities.

"Genius" is being flexible and changing directions when something unexpected happens.

"Genius" is knowing that luck and timing are part of the process.

"Genius" is being curious and always asking questions.

"Genius" is never taking no for an answer.

> "Name the greatest of all inventors. **Accident.**"
> —Mark Twain, author

All the accidental geniuses we profile in this book share these and other personal qualities. These amazing innovators come from diverse backgrounds, religions and countries. Some were successful when they were young. Some took years to come up with an invention or make a discovery. Some worked alone while others collaborated with colleagues.

But each one has made a difference in the world. Each one pursued work they loved with passion, curiosity, **tenacity** and a little luck.

You never know! One day you too may become an accidental genius!

> "Anyone who has never made a mistake has never tried anything new."
> —Albert Einstein, scientist

> "Somewhere, something incredible is waiting to be known."
> —Carl Sagan, scientist

CHAPTER ONE
DON'T BE AFRAID TO TRY

Successful innovators try different experiments on the road to an amazing discovery or useful invention. If one experiment doesn't work, they try another until they've exhausted all possibilities. Then they try again.

Sometimes prizes propel inventors to try something new. In the early eighteenth century General Napoleon Bonaparte of France had trouble getting fresh food for his troops. He offered a prize to anyone who could figure out a way to keep food fresh while it was being transported.

For years chef Nicolas Appert had pondered different ways to solve that problem, but Napoleon's prize spurred him on to work even harder. Appert's solution? Heating, boiling and sealing food in airtight glass jars! Although his innovation won him Napoleon's prize, the jars broke easily, so they didn't work out as well as he'd hoped. Still, it was an important first step in solving the food-storage problem and led to the invention of the tin can by Philippe de Girard and Peter Durand.

> "An inventor fails 999 times, and if he succeeds once, he's in. He treats his failures as simply practice shots."
>
> —Charles F. Kettering, inventor and engineer

Chemist Robert Chesebrough made **kerosene** from sperm whale oil. But when the discovery of petroleum made the need for kerosene **obsolete,** Chesebrough decided to learn more about this new fuel. He found that the sticky goo that accumulated around oil-pump rods was also useful for healing cuts and burns. He experimented with the substance for ten years, until he felt it was just right, and in 1872 **patented** it with the name Vaseline (see page 87 for more about patents). Then Chesebrough traveled around selling and promoting his product. Vaseline is still used widely all around the world.

What can I do with this stuff?
In his laboratory, Leo Baekeland
checks out the substance he
accidentally created.

FROM SHELLAC TO SENSATIONAL

Plastic, 1909

Dr. Leo Hendrik Baekeland

(1863–1944)

How did Leo Baekeland, the son of a Belgian shoemaker and a maid, become the "father of plastics"?

As a boy, when he read about scientists and inventors like Benjamin Franklin, Baekeland wanted to invent something amazing too. So he studied hard at school and won scholarships. And, like Franklin, he never gave up, even when things didn't work out the way he expected.

His mother also encouraged him to excel, and by the time Baekeland was twenty-one he'd earned a PhD in chemistry.

In 1889 Baekeland, his wife, Celine, and their three children moved to the United States, where Baekeland invented Velox, a new type of photographic paper. The Eastman Kodak Company bought Velox, and with the money Baekeland earned he bought a house and set up a laboratory at home. Now it was time to invent something else!

Is it a rocket ship? Is it a robot? No! It's the original Bakelizer—the machine used from 1901 to 1910 to make Bakelite.

Baekeland decided to create a cheaper form of shellac, a substance that was widely used to glaze food and treat wood. Shellac was made from the excretion of female lac bugs found in the forests of India and Thailand. You needed a lot of bugs—over 50,000 to make 1 kilogram (2.2 pounds) of shellac. That made it expensive.

But in trying to invent a new shellac, Baekeland accidentally created a different and surprising substance. This substance could be molded into different shapes before it hardened permanently. Baekeland called it Bakelite and in 1909 patented his invention. Soon there were Bakelite radios, cars, appliances and costume jewelry. Bakelite inspired a whole new industry—plastics.

A stylish Bakelite breadbox will not only keep your bread fresh but will also look good in your kitchen!

Bakelite jewelry is so colorful and elegant that even world-famous designer Coco Chanel admired and wore it.

UNBREAKABLE
Kevlar, 1971
Stephanie Kwolek
(1923–2014)

Chemist Stephanie Kwolek might have been the shortest person on her team of scientists, but she was big on great ideas!

When she was young, Stephanie Kwolek loved to spend time with her dad, exploring the natural world close to her home near Pittsburgh, Pennsylvania. That early interest inspired Stephanie to study chemistry in college. She was eager to find a science-related job and earn money to attend medical school. But in those days, few women worked in science.

Kwolek was lucky. World War II (1939–1945) had just ended, and many men were still overseas. Employers were glad to find a skilled worker, even if that worker *was* a woman. Kwolek found work with DuPont Company and liked her job so much she decided not to apply to medical school. Four years later, when her DuPont team moved to Delaware, Kwolek moved with it. In 1964 her team was busy looking for a lightweight yet strong fiber that could be used in making tires. They thought lighter tires would save on fuel.

Kwolek loved fabrics and once thought about becoming a fashion designer, but her love of chemistry led to her invention of a different kind of fabric—one that can stop bullets or keep a firefighter safe.

Above: *Kevlar is used to make bike tires, racing sails, bulletproof vests, diving suits and fireproof clothing.* Below: *Kevlar is unaffected by heat and is surprisingly light. Close up it looks like a honeycomb.*

"To invent you need a good imagination and a pile of junk."

—Thomas A. Edison, inventor

One day while experimenting, Kwolek produced a strange, cloudy concoction. Before her colleague could throw the murky mess out, Kwolek stopped him. She had a hunch. This solution might be good!

Tests proved she was right. Kwolek had accidentally developed a solution stronger than nylon or steel—only it wasn't quite right yet. Kwolek kept on experimenting, and in 1971 Kevlar was born.

Kevlar has been used to make tennis rackets, skis, boats, airplanes, cable tires, bulletproof vests, firefighter boots, hockey sticks and many more products.

Kwolek never made money on her invention. Her employer, DuPont, held the patent. But Kwolek was honored as the fourth woman ever to be inducted into the National Inventors Hall of Fame, and she earned many other awards.

Skis made with Kevlar won't crack as you fly over the snow.
Kevlar absorbs impacts and vibrations.

BLOW UP
Smart Dust, 2003

Jamie Link

(1978–)

In 2004 Jamie Link (center) was named to Technology Review's list of the world's 100 Top Young Innovators, along with Serge Belongie (left) and Lei Wang.

You never know what will happen when you enter a contest. Jamie Link, a twenty-five-year-old graduate student at the University of California, San Diego, won a $50,000 grand prize in the Collegiate Inventors Competition, a program of the National Inventors Hall of Fame. Her winning invention—"smart dust" made of **silicon**—happened by accident.

Link had always been interested in mathematics and science, especially chemistry. She studied chemistry first at Princeton and then at the University of California. That's where she accidentally broke a silicon chip, which stores electronic information. Instead of tossing the broken bits of chip in the garbage, Link examined them carefully. To her amazement, each of the tiny pieces—the silicon dust—looked and worked exactly like the original bigger chip.

5 mm

What did that mean? What could you do with it? Link realized that her accidental discovery had many practical applications. Scientists could use the smart dust particles to detect poisons in water and air or to screen chemicals in new drugs. Sensors in the dust would change color if there was something toxic in water, air or drugs.

Link was thrilled. Smart dust would help preserve precious resources like water. "I'm most excited about the environmental applications of smart dust," she said. "When I went down to Baja to test the polluted bay, I was shocked to see how dirty the water was. It made me realize how much we need tools like this."

Tiny but mighty smart dust changes color in water to detect poisons and pollutants.

CHAPTER TWO
GET KNOWLEDGE AND USE IT

Once they've identified a problem, accidental geniuses acquire more knowledge, analyze **data** and use all that information to figure out a solution. These strategies especially help when an experiment fails or the results are unexpected.

So how do you get knowledge about a problem?

You observe. You listen. You consult others. You read everything on the subject that you can.

All innovators benefit from the work of others. They know they might encounter failure. They know they might have to rethink their approach. But accidental geniuses are always open to new ideas and directions.

In the 1850s Whitcomb Judson invented the "clasp locker," or zipper, after being inspired by an early fastener made by Elias Howe Jr., who invented the sewing machine. Judson showed his clasp locker at the Chicago World's Fair in 1893, but no one was interested or could see a purpose for his clumsy product. A few years later Gideon Sundback, a Swedish-born electrical engineer, threw himself into improving and perfecting Judson's design. By December 1913 Sundback had developed the modern zipper. In 1917 he got a patent for it and made machinery to produce it. The zipper began to take off—at least on boots. It took about twenty more years for zippers to appear on clothing and many other products.

> **"It is possible to fly without motors, but not without knowledge and skill."**
>
> —Wilbur Wright,
> co-inventor of the airplane

THE MAID DID IT

Classifying Stars, 1890

Williamina Paton Stevens Fleming

(1857–1911)

Scottish-born Williamina Fleming found work as a housekeeper when her husband left her after they'd moved to Boston, Massachusetts, and before her son was born. Although she was smart and liked science and math, in her day there were few job possibilities for women besides becoming a teacher, seamstress or housekeeper. And single mothers had even fewer choices.

Luckily Fleming found work with Edward Pickering, a professor of astronomy at Harvard and the director of the Harvard College Observatory. Pickering had high standards and demanded excellence, and Fleming was excellent at her job. She was so good, and he was so frustrated with his assistant astronomers, he is reported to have said that his Scottish maid would do a better, more thorough job than his male assistants. Soon thereafter, Pickering hired Williamina Fleming to do just that.

Fleming proved her boss right. She studied, worked carefully and diligently, and **classified** 10,351 stars into 17 categories. She discovered 10 novae, stars whose light suddenly increases and then fades. She discovered 59 gaseous nebulae or dust clouds. She studied long-period **variable stars** and identified 222 of them.

At first her name didn't appear on the published reports of her work, but by 1890 it did. And Fleming continued to hire other smart, science-minded women to become astronomers, many of whom became world famous.

> **"The art and science of asking questions is the source of all knowledge."**
> —Thomas Berger, writer

Above: *By studying and following the stars, Williamina Fleming (right) and her colleagues helped us understand our universe.* Below: *In 1888 Fleming recorded the Horsehead nebula (dust clouds in the space between the stars) on a photographic plate at the Harvard College Observatory. Now you can see the nebula, which looks like a horse's head when seen from Earth, through the Hubble Space Telescope.*

AMAZING RADIATION

X-Rays, 1895

Dr. Wilhelm Röntgen
(1845–1923)

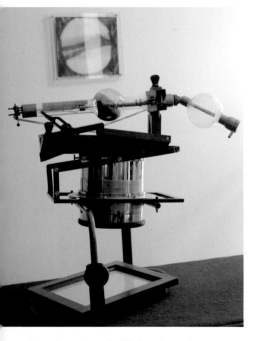

An early version of Wilhelm Röntgen's amazing, lifesaving discovery, on display at the Röntgen Memorial Site in Würzburg, Germany.

If Wilhelm Röntgen hadn't stuck with his studies even after he was unfairly expelled from a technical school for drawing a funny picture of a teacher, he wouldn't have gotten a PhD in engineering. If he hadn't been good at designing mechanical objects, he might not have experimented with tubes, plates and screens. If his wife Anna's hand hadn't accidentally become part of his experiment, he might not have taken the first X-ray.

Röntgen was born in Germany, grew up in the Netherlands and became a professor of physics in Germany. Along the way he studied the work of other scientists, especially their work on **electric currents** passing through gas at very low pressure. Röntgen did his experiments in a dark room, wrapping a tube with black cardboard and shutting out all light.

He moved equipment around to see what would happen. He watched, analyzed and tried new approaches. And when his wife put her hand in front of a **cathode ray**, he was astonished. Shadows showed the bones in her hands so clearly that he could see her wedding ring. It was such a startling skeletal image that Anna exclaimed, "I have seen my death!" Röntgen called the rays "X" for the unknown.

That first image would lead to a technology that diagnoses diseases early and saves lives. It didn't take long for other scientists to recognize the importance of Röntgen's discovery. He was awarded the first Nobel Prize in Physics (a top award—see page 89) in 1901.

AHA!

How the Curies Saved Lives

Marie Curie, who won two Nobel Prizes in science, was influenced by Röntgen's work. With her daughter Irène she brought X-ray machines close to the battle front in World War I to help diagnose wounded soldiers.

Wow! Is that me? The spooky way we all look on an X-ray.

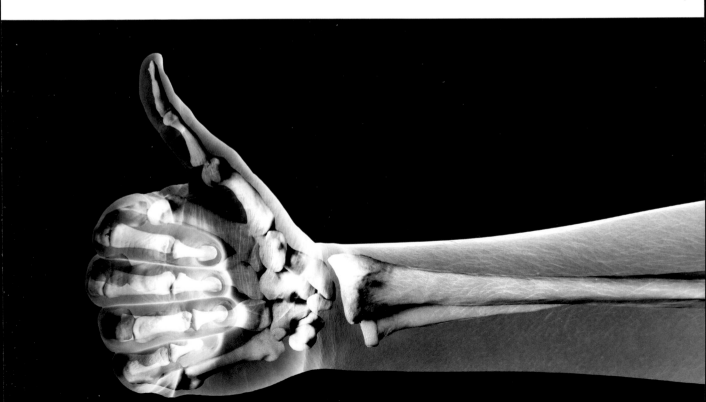

KEEP THAT BEAT GOING
Pacemakers, 1949

Dr. Wilfred G. Bigelow
(1913–2005)

Dr. John C. Callaghan
(1923–2004)

Wilfred Bigelow, John Callaghan and John Hopps team up to cut a ribbon opening a new technology center in Ontario.

Back in 1949 no one had ever performed open-heart surgery. Wilfred Bigelow of the Banting Institute in Toronto, Ontario, believed that's what you had to do to help some heart patients survive. But how could you keep a heart beating while performing open-heart surgery? After studying the importance of temperature in surgery, Bigelow and his colleague, John Callaghan, decided to try something new. They'd "super cool" a heart before they performed heart surgery. Unfortunately, when they did, the heart unexpectedly stopped. Bigelow tried cardiac massage, but that didn't work. "Out of desperation, I gave the heart a poke," he said. To his surprise, the electric probe he used made the heart start again. The patient recovered.

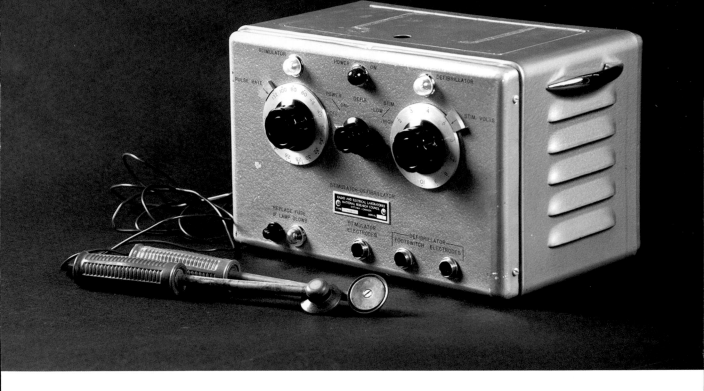

Now all the doctors had to do was turn this accidental discovery into a device to zap damaged hearts. They'd need an electrical engineer to build that device. They found Dr. John Hopps, and he built the first pacemaker. It was bigger than a shoebox, which limited its use, but eventually other medical inventors created a much smaller version that could be inserted directly into a person's chest.

John Hopps had a pacemaker implanted in his own heart in 1984. He lived fourteen more years.

External cardiac pacemaker-defibrillator invented by John Hopps and built by Ray Charbonneau.

AMAZING *and* TRUE

LUCKY ACCIDENT!

Wilson Greatbatch invented the implantable pacemaker in 1956 while building a heart-rhythm recording device and accidentally installing the wrong part.

CHAPTER THREE
PAY ATTENTION

Inventors create things to make life better, easier or more fun. Inventions can also help make things cheaper or make them work faster. So successful accidental geniuses stay aware of what's happening around them.

In 1994, ten-year-old Kathryn "KK" Gregory was playing in the snow outside her home in Bedford, Massachusetts. She became bone-chillingly cold and wet when snow went up her coat sleeves. Brrr! But, unlike most people, Gregory did something about it. She invented polar-fleece fingerless gloves she called Wristies.

Gregory's invention was so successful that she created Wristies that musicians can wear when they're practicing. The gloves keep their hands warm and flexible. Another style of Wristie even has a pocket for a hand warmer.

Sometimes an inventor needs to pay special attention when his work gives him a surprising result. William Henry Perkin was an English chemist. In 1856 he was trying to make artificial quinine to treat malaria, a disease that causes high fevers.

When Perkin instead created a substance with a strong purple color, he realized he'd created the first artificial (manufactured) dye. He called it mauveine, or mauve, and it led to many new colors and dyes.

AHA!

Small but Necessary

Sometimes inventors have to pay careful attention to small things. For instance, in the first half of the 1900s everyone loved sipping drinks from cans. There was just one problem—people needed an opener to pop open the cans.

On a picnic in 1959, American inventor Ermal Fraze left his opener at home. He had to use a car bumper to open a can. How frustrating! Fraze figured there had to be a better way, and a few months later he began working on what would become the ring pull, or pull tab. Opening pop cans was now much easier.

> "Concentrate all your thoughts upon the work at hand."
> —Alexander Graham Bell, inventor of the telephone

CLEAN SWEEP

Windshield Wipers, 1903

Mary Anderson

(1866–1953)

Mary Anderson was riding on a cold, wet streetcar like this one when inspiration hit.

O h, that poor streetcar driver, thought Mary Anderson. She was visiting New York City in November 1902, and the weather was terrible. Sleet drizzled down, and the driver couldn't see out the windows of his trolley car. He had to keep the front window open. Icy wet snow flew in his face and soaked him.

The other passengers on the streetcar must have seen the sleet pouring in on the driver, but only Anderson really paid attention. When she returned to her home in Alabama, she thought about the problem some more and invented the windshield wiper.

With Anderson's invention, a lever inside the vehicle moved an arm attached to a rubber blade on the outside. The driver turned the lever by hand to make the arm sweep back and forth across the windshield.

A **counterweight** on the lever kept the wiper in contact with the window.

Other inventors had come up with similar devices, but Anderson's was the first to really work. In the beginning, people thought the wipers would distract drivers. But as more people started driving cars, windshield wipers became standard.

Another female inventor, Charlotte Bridgwood, also paid attention. She saw the need for automatic windshield wipers—ones drivers could operate with just a flick of a switch—which she invented in 1917.

Not Another Broken Dish!

Another female inventor who paid attention to what was needed was Josephine Cochrane. It was her frustration with servants chipping and breaking plates that drove her to become an inventor. "If nobody else is going to invent a dishwashing machine," Cochrane said, "I'll do it myself!"

So, with the help of a mechanic named George Butters, Cochrane created the first practical dishwasher. It included wire racks and pressurized water, like today's machines. Her friends were soon clamoring for dishwashers of their own. Although Cochrane died in 1913, she was made a member of the National Inventors Hall of Fame in 2006.

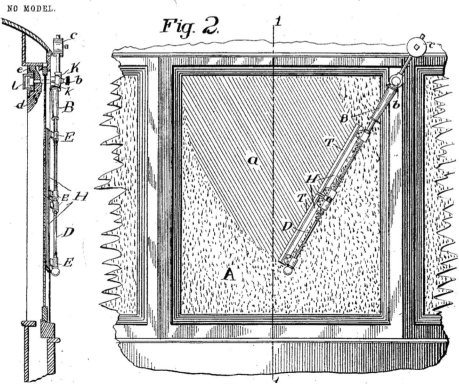

M. ANDERSON.
WINDOW CLEANING DEVICE.
APPLICATION FILED JUNE 18, 1903.

NO MODEL.

Fig. 2.

When Anderson filed for the patent on her windshield wiper in 1903, her application had to include detailed drawings of her invention.

NUTS TO YOU
Plenty of Peanut Products, 1910s

George Washington Carver

(1860s–1943)

George Washington Carver dried and prepared these samples of peanut plants. The peanut is a strange plant. After it flowers, its stalks send "pegs" burrowing down into the soil. There each tip swells to become a peanut shell.

As a boy, George Washington Carver was already interested in plants. In the mid-1880s, when Carver was about twenty, he applied to attend a college in Kansas, where he was living. He was proud to be accepted, but when he showed up, he was turned away. That's because the college didn't accept black students like Carver. He never forgot how bad that made him feel.

Carver eventually studied botany (the science of plants) at Iowa State College. He graduated in 1894 and became Iowa State's first African American teacher. When Tuskegee Normal and Industrial Institute in Alabama offered Carver a job, he jumped at it. ("Normal Institute" is another name for a school where people learn to become teachers. Today the school is called Tuskegee University.) This college was for black students.

Carver was a professor as well as an accidental genius and inventor. His students loved him—but Carver preferred working in his lab to lecturing.

Above: *Carver created peanut products that people could eat, and he also made creams, lotions and oils like these. Some were created by the Carvoline Company, named after Carver. Below: Peanuts are still an important crop across the southern United States. Here's a Natural Resources Conservation Service employee discussing peanuts with a farmer in Florida.*

Carver saw how poor the black farmers in Alabama were and wanted to help them. Many grew cotton, which takes more **nutrients** out of the soil than almost any other crop. The soil the farmers were working produced less cotton every year as the soil got worse.

Growing peanuts was Carver's solution. Why? Because they actually enrich the soil and also yield crops people can eat. Farmers took George's advice, and soon there were a lot of peanuts on the market. Carver paid attention and decided it was up to him to invent uses for all those extra peanuts.

So Carver locked himself in his lab and began work. Shampoo, gasoline, fruit punch, chili sauce—these are just a few of the more than 325 peanut products Carver created.

During the 1930s Carver toured the United States, speaking about peanuts and agriculture at colleges for white students, farmers' conferences and state fairs. His hard work and genius made white people realize how intelligent black people could be and helped change the way they were treated. He died in 1943 but was elected to the National Inventors Hall of Fame in 1990.

Lots of people call peanuts "goobers." That name comes from the African word n-guba. Peanuts are one of the world's oldest crops. They're small, but they changed Carver's life and transformed farming in the southern United States.

Carver didn't just invent. Another way he helped farmers was by holding talks about plants. Many of the farmers couldn't attend Carver's lectures, so he sent experts out in this truck to visit the farmers.

Since 1979 George Washington Carver Science Fairs have helped students like this girl learn about science and inventing.

THE ACCIDENT THAT STILL SAVES MILLIONS

Penicillin, 1928

Sir Alexander Fleming

(1881–1955)

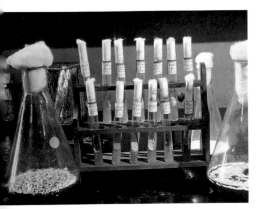

After Alexander Fleming accidentally discovered penicillin, he used flasks and test tubes like these to develop it and help make it available to patients.

Scottish scientist Alexander Fleming was brilliant—and *very* messy! So when he left his lab at St. Mary's Hospital in London, England, for a holiday in August 1928, he didn't tidy up the **bacteria** samples he was growing.

When Fleming got back to work, he discovered that **mold** spores had fallen into an uncovered dish of bacteria. Uh-oh! Now he would have to start his experiment all over again. He picked up the dish to throw it away—and then he took a second look, paying close attention to what he saw.

Fleming noticed that where the mold had landed, it had killed the bacteria around it. What was going on? Fleming grew a sample of the mold and discovered it gave off a bacteria-killing liquid. At first he called it

"mold juice," but he later renamed it "penicillin" after the *Penicillium notatum* (now known as *Penicillium chrysogenum*) mold that produced it.

Penicillin changed medicine. It was one of the first **antibiotics**—bacteria killers—that scientists discovered. By the 1940s scientists were able to **mass-produce** it. Now drug companies know how to make **synthetic** penicillin, which makes the drug available to even more people.

Experts estimate that penicillin and other antibiotics have saved more than 200 million lives. As Fleming said, "One sometimes finds what one is not looking for." But that's only true for inventors who pay attention!

Those fuzzy blue spots on these petri dishes are penicillin fungi.

microwaves

Folding Beds

Velcro

S. E. GOODE
No. 322,177. CABINET BED.
Fig. 1 Patented July 14, 1885.

CHAPTER FOUR
MAKE CONNECTIONS

Wise inventors and scientists analyze what's been done in the past to help them discover something new. They're always alert and open to new possibilities and new products.

In 1877 Thomas Edison was trying to invent a telegraph transmitter. While he was fiddling with the transmitter he noticed that the machine's tape gave off an odd noise when it was played at high speed. It sounded like people speaking! That gave Edison a *new* idea—maybe he could record a message.

His experiments led him to try recording sound on tinfoil-covered cylinders. When Edison spoke into the mouthpiece, the vibrations of his voice were indented into the cylinder by a needle. And when he played it back by cranking a long shaft, he heard his own words: "Mary had a little lamb." Edison was excited! He was sure that this new invention, a foil phonograph, was going to be a big hit. There would be so many uses for it, like taking dictation, recording family voices, building clocks that announced the time and listening to music someone had previously played. Edison was so convinced of the possibilities of the phonograph that he started a company to sell it the very next year. He was right. The tinfoil phonograph delighted the public and the scientific community, but it took Edison another ten years to produce a better version using wax cylinders for recording.

"Minds are like parachutes—they only function when open."

—Thomas Dewar, businessman

IT MAKES SENSE

Folding Beds, 1885

Sarah E. Goode

(1855–1905)

How do you cope if your apartment is so small you barely have room for a bed and there's little storage space? That was a problem many people faced, especially in a big city like Chicago, where Sarah Goode and her family lived. Goode knew a lot about furniture. Her father was a carpenter, and her husband, Archie, upholstered chairs and sofas and built stairs. Goode was determined to do something to help their customers with storage and space. She considered three things:

1. The bed had to fold and unfold easily.
2. It had to be strong enough to support the weight of a person.
3. It had to stay in place and not move around.

INVENTION

A Spotlight on Early African-American Inventions

The Cabinet Bed
by Sarah E. Goode

U.S. Patent No. 322,177 • July 14, 1885

This dual purpose space saving furniture could fold into a desk or unfold into a bed.

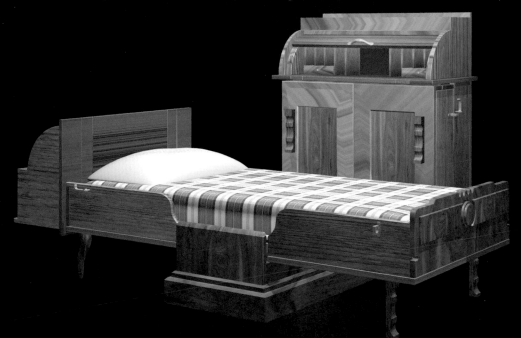

When folded as a desk a roll-top cover was used to enclose the shelf and cabinet area. Sarah used a pair of metal brackets to pivot and roll the cover in opened and closed positions.

Integrated beneath the shelf area was a sliding writing board which pulled out for use and slid back when done. The latches on the side of the desk kept the desk from unfolding during use.

To allow the cabinet to unfold Sarah designed two folding parts sitting on a base which were held together with metal arms. In the center of the bed was a spring support. This tray of springs supported the user's back when lying down.

To make handling the folding sections easy Sarah installed a counter-balance system using flexible flat metal rods. This made the sections lighter. The rods were anchored on one end and made to slide freely on the other for opening and closing.

Sarah E. Goode is known as the first African-American woman to be awarded a patent by the United States government. Her Cabinet Bed proudly takes its place among earlier American dual-purpose furniture designs. Like others, it's a space saver in the home or office. Unlike others space savers that "hide-away", Sarah's Cabinet Bed transforms into a totally different and functional furniture item.

SMITH LENOIR
GRAPHIC CREATIONS

She invented a cabinet with strong **hinged** sections, one on either side, that could be pulled open to reveal a bed. When the bed was folded back up, the cabinet could be used as a desk, complete with space for stationery and other supplies. Goode solved two storage and space problems with just one piece of furniture! On July 14, 1885, she became one of the first African American women to receive a patent for an invention. Sarah Goode's bed became the basis for the Murphy bed, which was patented in 1900 and is still used today.

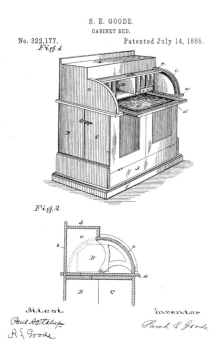

S. E. GOODE.
CABINET BED.
No. 322,177.   Patented July 14, 1885.

Above: A diagram from Goode's patent for the folding bed.

Left: If Sarah Goode knew how her folding-bed idea influenced later designs, such as the Murphy bed, she would be astonished. Below: Goode is remembered and honored by a school named after her. This academy encourages students to focus on STEM subjects (science, technology, engineering and math).

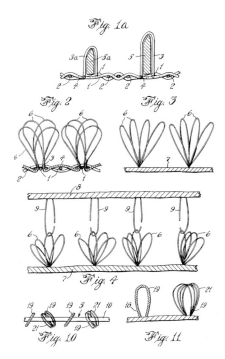

A WALK IN THE WOODS

Velcro, 1941

George de Mestral

(1907–1990)

In the 1960s George de Mestral took out a patent for Velcro. Few people knew what it was or what it could be used for in those days. Today Velcro is everywhere!

What do you do if you're out in the Swiss Alps with your dog and you find burrs stuck to your woolen socks, your jacket and your dog's fur?

You pull the burrs off when you return home, of course, but if you're an inventor like George de Mestral, you also start thinking. Maybe there's something useful in those sticky burrs.

De Mestral examined the burrs under a microscope and noticed they were made of hundreds of natural "hooks" that attached themselves to fabric. Now all he needed was a way to reproduce the burr effect with fibers. But that's where he ran into trouble. First he tried to use cotton to recreate the burr effect, but that didn't work. Then he tried nylon. It made good hooks but not the right size of loops. De Mestral was discouraged.

He was about to give up when he tried one more thing—trimming the loops. Hooray! Success! The only problem now was how to mechanize this process to create a product with practical uses. And what practical use would this new product have anyway?

It took de Mestral another eighteen years to work out all the kinks in his burr-inspired invention, which he called Velcro—a combination of *velours* (the French word for "velvet") and *crochet* (which means "hook"). He was granted a patent for Velcro in 1955, but the product didn't become popular until years later. It finally took off, thanks to the aerospace industry. Velcro helped astronauts get in and out of their bulky spacesuits. And that was just the beginning of its success.

Velcro's hook-and-loop design makes it a useful fastener for clothing, medical apparatuses and much more.

"Nature is the source of all true knowledge. She has her own logic, her own laws, she has no effect without cause nor invention without necessity."

—Leonardo da Vinci, inventor and artist

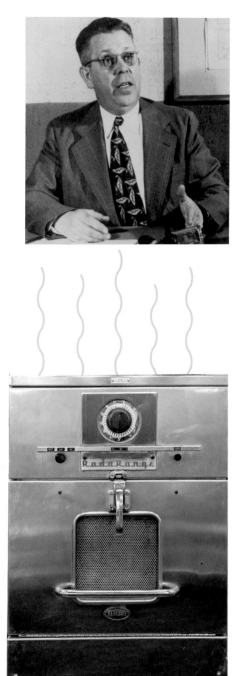

HOT POCKETS

Microwaves, 1945

Percy Spencer
(1894–1970)

Yikes! Too heavy and too big to use easily, this early microwave didn't sell.

How did a candy bar lead to the invention of the microwave? It all started with Percy Spencer, a self-taught engineer who became interested in **wireless communications** after reading about wireless operators on the *Titanic*. When Spencer entered the US Navy at age eighteen, he became a wireless expert by teaching himself advanced math, chemistry, physics and **metallurgy**.

By 1939 Spencer was one of the world's experts on **radar** tube design, working at Raytheon, a contractor for the US Department of Defense. His work on magnetrons, which were used to generate microwave radio signals, was vital for winning World War II. It was while working on magnetrons that Spencer noticed that a candy bar he'd left in his pocket had melted. He realized that heat from the magnetrons had caused the chocolate to melt very quickly. What would this heat do to other foods? Would popcorn pop? Yes! What about an egg? Yikes! When the egg was put near the magnetron, it cooked so fast that it exploded in a co-worker's face!

In 1945 Raytheon patented Spencer's invention, and two years later it built a commercial microwave oven, which weighed 750 pounds! It wasn't until years later, when the microwave oven was built much smaller, that it began selling like hotcakes. Unfortunately, Spencer never received royalties for the invention many households now consider an essential appliance (Raytheon owned the patent).

Once microwaves became smaller and sleeker, they flew out of the stores and into kitchens around the world.

AHA!

All About Bags

In 1926, when Laura Scudder saw that potato chips at her potato-chip factory quickly went stale in barrels, she had her workers create wax paper bags to wrap the chips in. The chips stayed fresh much longer. Scudder was also the first to put dates on the bags to let customers know how long food would stay fresh.

CHAPTER FIVE
RECOGNIZE THAT IT TAKES TIME

Inventors and scientists know it can take years, even decades, before their experiments are successful or show usable results. Accidental geniuses keep working, assessing their results and looking for the next step, no matter how long it takes.

"Don't be afraid of hard work. Nothing worthwhile comes easily," said Gertrude Elion, who won a Nobel Prize in Medicine in 1988 along with George Hitchings. Together they discovered drugs to treat **leukemia** and **herpes** and help prevent the body's rejection of foreign tissue in kidney transplants. Elion knew how long and hard you have to work to be accepted in your field, especially as a woman. Over the years she had to work as a lab assistant, a food analyst checking out berries and pickles, and a high-school teacher while completing a master's degree in chemistry at night. She was the only woman to graduate in chemistry in her class. And at first she couldn't find work as a chemist because she was a woman. But when many men were called up to fight in World War II, Elion got a job as an assistant to George Hitchings at Burroughs Wellcome, a drug company. She worked hard and kept learning, asking questions, analyzing data and thinking about problems.

She knew that every discovery takes time, patience and an openness to unexpected possibilities. She believed that what really mattered was not a prize, no matter how big, but the difference her work would make in people's lives. "The satisfaction of that is much greater than any prize you can get," she said.

REMEMBER THE ICE

Popsicles, 1905

Frank Epperson

(1894–1983)

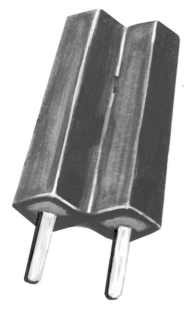

On a cold winter night in California in 1905, eleven-year-old Frank Epperson made a soft drink with fruit-flavored soda powder and water. But instead of drinking his concoction, Frank accidentally left it on the porch overnight with the stirring stick still in the glass. In the morning he discovered that the soda water had frozen solidly to the stick. He carefully removed his frozen drink from the glass. Then he tasted his accidental creation. To his delight, it tasted *good*.

Eighteen years later Epperson remembered his ice treat and decided to apply for a patent. He called his treat the Eppsicle, but that name didn't last. Some claim that his kids called Frank's treat the "Popsicle" after their dad. Others say it became known as a Popsicle because it was made from soda pop. Whatever the reason, the name Popsicle stuck. Frank experimented with different flavors for his frozen treat. In 1922, while he was selling real estate, he introduced the Popsicle at a firemen's ball. It was a hit!

In 1924 Epperson sold the rights to the Popsicle to the Joe Lowe Company in New York. Now the Popsicle really took off! When the twin Popsicle became available, that too became popular, because now two kids could split one treat.

Today we still love Popsicles, which come in many flavors. Frank's Popsicle has also influenced the invention of other frozen treats on a stick. Sadly, the double-stick version of the Popsicle is no longer made. It was eliminated in 1986 because many considered it too messy and clumsy to enjoy.

AHA!

Helping Grandma

At ten years old, when her grandmother was getting treatment for cancer, Sophie Broderick wanted to help her grandma feel better. So she invented the "Chemo Thera Pop," a nutrient-rich frozen dessert that relieves the pain from a sore mouth and helps patients who have lost their appetite.

There's nothing like licking a Popsicle on a hot summer day (or any day).

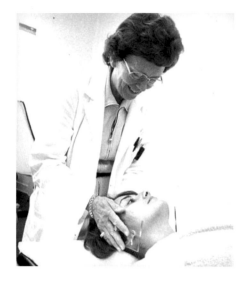

NIGHT AFTER NIGHT

High-Dose Radiation, 1949

Dr. Vera Peters

(1911–1993)

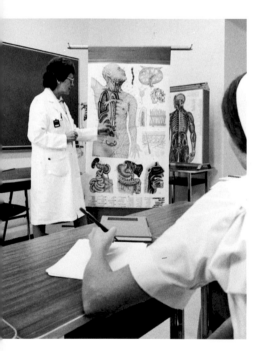

Vera Peters fought for everyone's health, but especially women's.

When Vera Peters was a girl in 1920s rural Ontario, she milked cows, drove tractors and dreamed that one day she'd become a doctor. Few women pursued medicine in those days, but with her mom's encouragement and her own determination, Peters was one of ten women out of a class of 115 who graduated from the University of Toronto's medical school in 1934. When her mom was diagnosed with breast cancer while Peters was in medical school, she explored all the available treatments for cancer, including **radiation**.

Although her mom died, Peters was determined to keep studying and analyzing data to prove that radiation could cure cancers. No matter how tired she was after a hard day's work at the medical clinic, she studied and analyzed at night. After two years of thorough,

exhausting work, she concluded that early-stage Hodgkin's disease (a type of cancer), incurable at the time, could be cured with high-dose radiation.

Her discovery changed the treatment for Hodgkin's patients. Now Peters was ready to work on another theory—this time for the treatment of breast cancer. She believed that radical surgery wasn't always the best answer for many breast-cancer patients. She studied and analyzed data until she was ready to share her results and insights. Her persistent and pioneering work eventually changed medical practices for fighting cancer. She made people think in new ways and gave patients new lifesaving treatment options.

Left to right: Anne Shepherd as a nurse and Helly Chester as Vera Peters in the hit play Radical.

AMAZING *and* TRUE

LINEUPS

Many people lined up to see Charles Hayter's play *Radical*, about Vera Peters, which opened in Toronto in 2014. The playwright—who is also a radiation **oncologist** (cancer specialist)—never imagined that Vera Peters's story would draw so many people.

STICK TO IT

Post-it Notes, 1980

Dr. Spencer Silver
(1941–)

Art Fry
(1931–)

Spencer Silver, co-inventor of the Post-it Note, called it "a product nobody thought they needed until they did." Silver was a chemist for the 3M Company, specializing in **adhesive** technology. Arthur Fry, who worked for 3M too but in product development, had a knack for finding new uses for things. The two men's collaboration started after Silver tried to create a super-strong glue for 3M. But in the 1960s Silver developed a not-so-strong, reusable adhesive instead of super glue. For years he tried to find a use for his temporary glue but with no success.

Then one day in 1974, Fry was looking for a bookmark that wouldn't pop out of his church hymnal and remembered Silver's reusable glue. He applied the glue to a piece of paper and stuck it in his hymnal. Perfect!

Fry shared his new use for Silver's glue with his colleague, and the men started leaving adhesive notes all around their office. Everyone loved them, including their bosses at 3M, who decided that this product could be marketed to the public. They first called the notes "Press 'n Peel," but the name wasn't popular. They finally relaunched them in 1980 as Post-it Notes, and consumers loved them. Today Post-it Notes are sold in more than 100 countries, and people have found multiple uses for the temporary adhesive notes.

Imagine the uses! You can do almost anything with Post-it Notes, from writing to your family and friends to creating superhero art.

"Invention is not enough. Tesla invented the electric power we use, but he struggled to get it out to people. You have to combine both things: invention and innovation focus, plus the company that can commercialize things and get them to people."

—Larry Page, co-founder of Google

Art Fry and Spencer Silver cheer on young inventors at the National Inventors Hall of Fame's Camp Invention.

Fiber Optics

ROCKET FUEL

TRAMPOLINE

69.48'

37.50

32.08

REDSTONE

JUPITER C

32.08

69.48'

69.90'

9.27'

9.27'

CHAPTER SIX
BE PERSISTENT

Great inventors know that the key to a successful result is to never give up. They have the drive to find answers, even if it takes many tries to complete their inventions.

Mandy Haberman, who created the Anywayup Cup in 1992, is a persistent inventor. This British **entrepreneur** couldn't get any stores to sell her no-spill cup for young kids. So Haberman mailed one of her cups—filled with liquid—to a store. Not a drop spilled! Whew! Now millions of her inventions are sold around the world. Haberman was named British Female Inventor of the Year in 2000.

Percy Shaw was driving home late one night in 1934. It was so dark he was having trouble seeing. Then he noticed his car lights being reflected in the eyes of a cat. He immediately had the idea for "cat's eyes" lights embedded in the road. But the English inventor had to persist and find ways to make his invention stand up to being driven over, as well as withstand road-cleaning and snow-clearing machinery.

AHA!

Goodyear's Good Idea

In the 1820s American Charles Goodyear became fascinated by things made of rubber. But the rubber that was available turned brittle when cold, and sticky when heated. So Goodyear began trying to create useful rubber.

In 1939 he spilled a rubber mixture on his hot stove. The mixture didn't melt and it stayed elastic when chilled. Goodyear called his process of heating a rubber-acid mixture "vulcanization" (Vulcan is the god of fire). Car tires, balls—even erasers!—are some of the things made with Goodyear's process.

> "Ninety-nine percent of the failures come from people who have the habit of making excuses."
> —George Washington Carver, botanist and inventor (see page 32).

BOUNCE! BOUNCE! BOUNCE!

Trampolines, 1936

George Nissen

(1914–2010)

Kids—even royal ones!—love jumping on trampolines. Here are Princesses Margarita and Maria Carolina of the Dutch royal family in 1980, playing on this accidental invention.

Trapeze artists fascinated George Nissen. In 1930, when he was just sixteen, he watched a group whirling through the air high above his head at a circus in his hometown in Iowa. But at the end of their routines, the athletes dropped from their swinging bars into the safety net below.

Nissen was a diver and a gymnast at his school. He thought how much more spectacular the show would be if the trapeze artists kept bouncing and flipping on the net.

When Nissen got home, he strapped a canvas sheet to a rectangular frame. But it wasn't very bouncy. Now what? Nissen connected the canvas to the frame using the inner tubes from tires. He called his invention the bouncing rig. Sadly for Nissen, it wasn't very successful.

But he didn't give up. After graduating from college, Nissen and some friends toured the United States and

Mexico, performing on the bouncing rig at fairs and carnivals. While in Mexico, he heard the Spanish word for springboard: *trampolín*. Nissen added an *e* to the end and renamed his invention the trampoline. Success!

During World War II, Nissen's creation was used to help pilots orient themselves in the air. Later, American astronauts and Soviet **cosmonauts** trained on trampolines.

Nissen also invented the game of Spaceball, a combo of basketball and volleyball played on a trampoline. But he dreamed of trampolining becoming an official Olympic sport. For years he wrote to sports officials to plead his case. Nissen's persistence paid off. At the 2000 Summer Olympic Games in Sydney, Australia, eighty-six-year-old Nissen watched proudly as athletes competed on the trampoline for the first time.

Above: Nissen (lower left) demonstrating the game of Spaceball. He always said it was his favorite invention. Below: Trampolines are great for exercising—the springy jumping surface reduces most of the stress on jumpers' joints. They're great for just having fun too!

Narinder Singh Kapany with an early version of a laparoscope, a fiber optic cable system. This device allows someone to view an area that's hard to get at by snaking the cable in from a more accessible spot. Kapany became known as the "Father of Fiber Optics."

LIGHT BENDER

Fiber Optics, 1954

Dr. Narinder Singh Kapany

(1926–)

When Narinder Singh Kapany was a high-school student in Dahradun, India, he got an idea that would change the world. He realized that light didn't have to travel in a straight line, that it could be bent. He just had to figure out how.

In 1952, when Kapany was twenty-five, he went to college in London, England, and decided to work on his light-bending idea using long thin strands, or fibers, of glass. First he had trouble getting glass fibers that were thin enough and had no impurities in them.

Once Kapany had thin fibers that were pure enough, he had to figure out a way to make bundles of the fibers work efficiently together. But he persisted and in 1954 succeeded in bending light using optical fibers—flexible, transparent strands of glass or plastic, each only a little thicker than a human hair.

Optical fiber cables transmit light over longer distances than electric cables do.

Kapany was the first to use the term *fiber optics*. Today, optical fibers are used in communications to transmit signals. They also allow doctors to look inside patients' bodies and help workers inspect hard-to-reach places, such as the interiors of jet engines.

Left: *Optical fibers are used mostly to transmit light from one end of the fiber to the other. Glass or plastic fibers are used instead of metal wires because signals travel along them better.* Below: *Kapany's invention has lots of uses. Optical fibers can transmit sunlight from the roof of a building to brighten other parts. These fibers can light up signs, art and even toys.*

AHA!

Connect the Dots

When Louis Braille was only three years old, he had an accident that left him blind. He loved to read, but in the early 1800s books for visually disabled people used raised letters that were hard to read.

Braille found out about a military code called night writing. Soldiers were supposed to use it to communicate silently and when there was no light. But the system was too difficult to learn.

It took Braille a few years to make a workable code, but by the time he was fifteen he'd invented Braille, an alphabet of raised dots that's still used today.

IT *IS* ROCKET SCIENCE

Rocket Fuel, 1957

Mary Sherman Morgan

(1921–2004)

You can see this Jupiter-C rocket at the National Air and Space Museum of the Smithsonian Institution in Washington, DC.

Mary Sherman Morgan grew up poor in North Dakota in the 1920s. Her parents didn't think school was important, but Morgan persisted in her dream of getting an education. She ran away from home to go to college.

At university Morgan studied chemistry. But before she could finish her degree, World War II broke out. Morgan was offered a factory job. She needed the money, so she took the job and soon found herself helping to manufacture explosives.

After the war ended in 1945, Morgan went to work at North American Aviation in California. Soon she was calculating how well new fuels could propel rockets. About 900 rocket scientists worked there, and she was the only woman. She was also one of the few without a college degree.

Thanks to Mary Sherman Morgan's invention of Hydyne fuel, Jupiter-C/Explorer 1 launched from Cape Canaveral, Florida, on January 31, 1958.

AMAZING *and* TRUE

IT'S TOUGH BEING A FEMALE INVENTOR

Hardly anybody has heard of Mary Sherman Morgan. Lots can't name any female inventors. Why are there so few?

Many people used to think inventing wasn't "ladylike." As well, in the early 1900s some people believed education drove women crazy! It was hard for female inventors to gain the know-how they needed.

Girls are now encouraged to study STEM subjects—science, technology, engineering and math. Those are the areas that produce the most inventions and patents.

About 100 years ago less than 1 percent of patents issued in the United States went to women. Today that number's closer to 10 percent. Let's hope it doesn't take another 100 years to reach 50 percent!

The United States was falling behind Russia in the space race. One big reason was that American rocket fuel wasn't effective enough to launch the rockets. It took years, but Morgan persisted with her work, and in 1957 she invented the fuel Hydyne. It powered the Jupiter-C rocket that put Explorer I, the first American satellite, into orbit.

Thanks to Morgan's persistence, she became known as "The Woman Who Saved the U.S. Space Race."

CHAPTER SEVEN

RECOGNIZE THAT FAILURE IS PART OF THE PROCESS

Famous inventor Thomas Edison once said, "I have not failed. I've just found 10,000 ways that won't work." Successful accidental geniuses understand this. They keep experimenting and inventing despite their failures.

Edison has become known as America's greatest inventor. He developed the phonograph (an early device for recording and playing music), the movie camera and a long-lasting lightbulb. He held more than 1,000 patents—and he had a lot of failures along the way.

But Edison never quit. "Many of life's failures," he said, "are people who did not realize how close they were to success when they gave up."

Sometimes inventors turn failure into success by changing how they see their invention. In 1957 Alfred Fielding and Marc Chavannes were trying to make textured wallpaper that was easy to clean. All their ideas failed—but they did discover that the wall covering could be used as packing material. Bubble wrap was born. Pop, pop, pop!

Some inventors go for a walk when they hit a roadblock. Others doodle. It always helps to keep a notebook so you've got a record of what you've tried and what doesn't work.

Successful inventors keep trying. "Our greatest weakness lies in giving up," Edison said. "The most certain way to succeed is always to try just one more time."

AHA!

Chilly Inspiration

Chester Greenwood was tired of his ears freezing when he skated with his friends. The 15-year-old convinced his grandmother to attach warm padding to a wire frame. He slipped his invention on his head, and finally his ears were warm.

Greenwood's friends made fun of him as he kept working on his invention. He had many failures with his attempts at other innovations, but now people around the world wear earmuffs.

IT'S IN THE BAG

Flat-Bottom Paper Bags, 1871

Margaret Knight

(1838–1914)

Margaret Knight knew that flat-bottomed paper bags were practical and could make packing and carrying much easier.

When Margaret Knight was growing up in Maine, she liked to invent and build things. Her father died when she was very young, and in 1850, when Knight was just twelve, she went to work in a cotton mill. She saw a worker get stabbed by a steel-tipped part of a loom (a weaving machine). So she quickly invented a safety device for looms.

Knight then began working for a company that made paper bags. At the time, flat-bottomed bags could only be made by hand, which was expensive. People usually used V-shaped bags, but they weren't nearly as useful.

For years people had tried to create a machine that would make flat-bottomed paper bags. Knight worked all day in the paper-bag factory and night after night tried to invent a new device. She made hundreds of models, but none worked. However, Knight learned from her mistakes. After many months she had finally created a design for the machine. Then it took two years for her to perfect it.

Knight's model of her design was built from wood. To get a patent she needed an iron version. While that was being made, a man saw it and stole Knight's idea. She took him to court and so impressed the judge with her knowledge that she won the case. Knight was awarded the patent for her machine in 1871. She started her own paper-bag company, and this patent was just the first of many for this innovator.

Knight's original bag-making machine is on display at the Smithsonian Institution in Washington, DC.

This is the model Knight used to apply for the patent for a paper-bag-folding machine. It's more than 140 years old, but the ideas behind it are still used to make paper bags!

AHA!

All-Purpose Perfect Product

The flat-bottomed paper bag is just one of many everyday products that took a lot of tries to get right.

The Rocket Chemical Company in San Diego, California, was trying to create a product that would repel moisture and prevent metals from rusting or **corroding**. Chemist Norman Larsen had already tried 39 options. It wasn't until trial number 40 in 1953 that he succeeded in creating a water-**displacing** (WD) chemical.

The company called the product WD-40. Today it's used to remove gum from carpets, unstick jammed zippers and loosen sticky locks—someone even used it to remove a python from under a bus!

Before antibiotics were discovered (see page 36), many people spent time in sanitariums, like this one the Kellogg brothers ran. There the patients recovered from various illnesses and diseases.

FLAKY INVENTORS

Kellogg's Corn Flakes, 1894

Dr. John Harvey Kellogg

(1852–1943)

Will Keith "W.K." Kellogg

(1860–1951)

John Harvey Kellogg (above) ran a sanitarium (a place where people go to recover after an illness) in Battle Creek, Michigan. He and his brother, Will Keith Kellogg, tried to provide healthy meals for their patients.

One day they accidentally left some boiled wheat sitting out for several hours, and it became dry and inedible. Yuck! They could have figured that the batch was a failure and just thrown it away. But their tight budget made them take another look at their mistake.

On that breakfast-changing day in August 1894, the brothers had been trying to find a substitute for bread that their patients could digest easily. When the brothers discovered the forgotten stale wheat,

The patients at the Kelloggs' sanitarium not only ate healthy food but also did breathing excercises like these.

Many famous and rich people stayed at the Battle Creek Sanitarium. Mary Todd Lincoln, wife of former American president Abraham Lincoln, visited this health resort.

they decided to continue processing it to see what happened. They forced it through rollers, thinking it would turn into long sheets of dough.

Instead the mixture broke off into flakes. The brothers were surprised, but they toasted the flakes and served them to their patients. Yum! The flakes were so popular that patients wanted to take them home.

Then W.K. got the idea of using corn instead of wheat to make the cereal. Corn flakes were even more popular. But W.K. believed the taste could be improved—he thought the cereal tasted like cardboard. When W.K. added sugar to the recipe in 1906, sales really took off. For many years Kellogg's Corn Flakes was one of the top-selling cereals around the world.

Corn Flakes is a catchy name for this popular cereal. But the Kelloggs called their first cereal flakes Granose. Today people in more than 180 countries eat Corn Flakes.

ZOOM!
The Razor Scooter, 1998

Gino Tsai

(1957–)

AHA!

From Stain Remover to Toy

Many famous accidental inventions involve sports equipment and toys.

For instance, before the 1940s, coal was used to heat homes. But it left stains on the wallpaper in homes, so American Noah McVicker created a doughy material to remove the marks. However, when natural gas became a more common—and cleaner—heat source, the dough stopped selling. Uh-oh. The invention now seemed like a failure.

In 1955, Noah's nephew, Joe McVicker, found out from his schoolteacher sister-in-law, Kay Zufall, that her students loved playing with the dough. Kay suggested Joe rename his invention Play-Doh, and it's still one of the world's most popular toys.

Mechanical engineer Gino Tsai was tired of it taking so long for him to get around his huge bicycle factory in Changhua, Taiwan. He felt his short legs slowed him down. So he decided to invent something that would speed up his life.

Scooters had been around for decades, but Tsai wanted to invent an all-new version. However, he and his team had to accept that failure can be part of the process of creating any invention. It took them five years of designing and experimenting, but Tsai and his team never gave up.

In 1998 the Razor scooter was finally ready to zoom Tsai around his factory. This modern scooter uses aluminum that's light but strong enough to be used in airplanes. The scooter also folds in half, so it's easy to store, and the scooter's handle can be adjusted to suit the height of any rider. No wonder more than five million Razor scooters sold in its first six months. It was named Toy of the Year in 2001.

Gino Tsai invented his scooter to help him at work. But today most of his scooters are used by kids having fun.

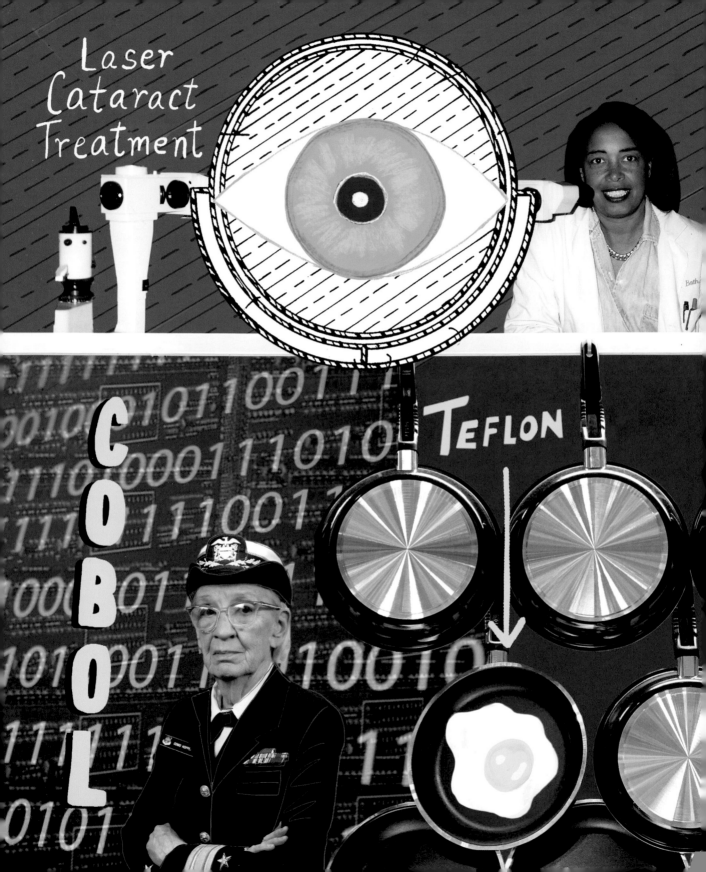

Laser Cataract Treatment

COBOL

TEFLON

CHAPTER EIGHT
DON'T MAKE ASSUMPTIONS

It's vital for accidental geniuses to use only information they know is correct or can check. No matter how tough it is to gather the data, or how much time it takes, successful inventors know how important this is.

Top inventors don't rely on hunches or guesses either. Instead of having their minds made up about their experiment results, these creators are open-minded.

For years, many inventors, including Orville and Wilbur Wright, tried to create the first airplane. The Wright brothers had built gliders but couldn't move beyond that.

The brothers knew they were using the same data other inventors had used about how air moves over wings. Was that the problem? In 1901 Orville and Wilbur stopped assuming these numbers were correct. The brothers built a wind tunnel to collect their own information. The Wrights discovered the old data was, well, not right! In 1903, after basing their work on their new results, they became the first men to fly.

AHA!

Rust Resistant

Harry Brearley was trying to create a better quality of steel for guns, so their barrels wouldn't wear away as quickly. This English scientist had experimented with different types of steel but had gotten nowhere. He began to try adding varying amounts of chromium to the steel.

On August 13, 1913, Brearley tested his latest steel by **etching** it with **nitric acid** and examining it by microscope to see how it stood up to the chemical. Brearley didn't assume he knew what the results would be. But this time he found that his new steel wasn't affected by wear or chemicals. He called it "rustless steel," and it later became known as **stainless steel**.

> **"If we all worked on the assumption that what is accepted as true is really true, there would be little hope of advance."**
>
> —Orville Wright, co-inventor of the airplane

NO STICK

Teflon, 1938

Dr. Roy J. Plunkett
(1910–1994)

Model of what scientists think polytetrafluoroethylene molecules look like.

What's going on? thought chemist Roy J. Plunkett. He was working in a lab in New Jersey in the 1930s, trying to create new types of refrigerants. They're the substances in refrigerators that help keep things cool. The refrigerants being used were poisonous and very explosive. Plunkett was trying to find a safer substitute.

One substance Plunkett was experimenting with was tetrafluoroethylene (TFE). On the morning of April 6, 1938, he and his assistant, Jack Rebok, opened the valve of a cylinder of TFE they'd been using the day before. They were amazed to find that nothing came out of the cylinder, even though its weight showed it was full.

Plunkett could have assumed his work was a failure. Instead he carefully tipped the cylinder upside down, and out came a waxy white powder. What was it?

It wasn't long before Plunkett realized that the TFE had formed a polymer. That means **molecules** had

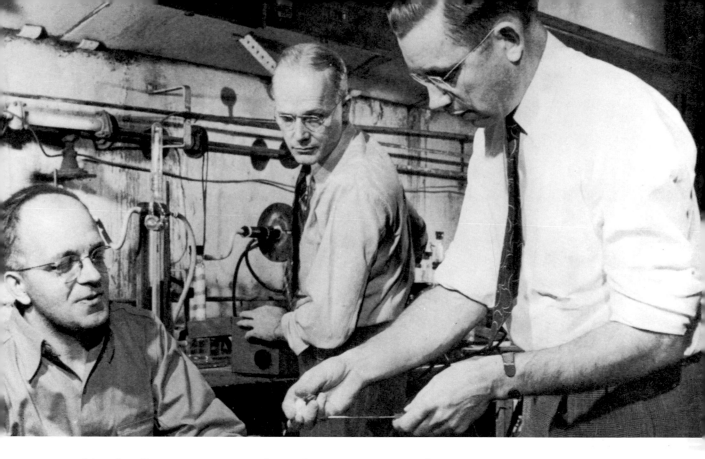

combined to form a more complex substance. He named it polytetrafluoroethylene (PTFE). Plunkett soon found that the PTFE didn't corrode (get eaten away by chemicals) and was extremely slippery. As well, PTFE could withstand high heat.

Three years later Plunkett's lab patented his discovery. They also gave it a new name that was easier for most people to pronounce: Teflon. The name is made up of letters from the original name—poly*tetra*f*l*uoroethyl*e*ne.

Today most people have a Teflon pan in the kitchen, because the pans are so easy to clean. Teflon is also used to coat machine parts to help them last longer. It's sprayed on carpets and furniture to repel stains, and it insulates data communication cables and weatherproofs outdoor signs.

Roy Plunkett (right) was working with Jack Rebok (left) and Robert McHarness when he discovered Teflon. Most polymer products weren't found by accident, but Plunkett had the smarts to recognize he'd found something new.

Teflon surfaces are so nonstick that liquids form beads on them.

CODE WORDS

COBOL, 1952

Dr. Grace Hopper

(1906–1992)

Growing up in the early 1900s in New York City, Grace Hopper was curious about everything around her. At age seven she decided to find out how clocks work. So she took apart every alarm clock in her house!

When Hopper grew up, she became a math professor. During World War II she joined the United States Navy Reserve (Navy staff who don't usually take part in battles). Grace wasn't allowed to join the Navy because she was thirty-four, which was considered too old.

After the war Hopper started work at a computer company. She helped develop the UNIVAC I, one of the first large-scale electronic computers. Then she began work on a computer program.

Everyone else assumed that computer programming languages had to be in code. They said computers didn't understand English. But Hopper didn't make that assumption. In 1952 she and her team invented the first compiler for computer languages.

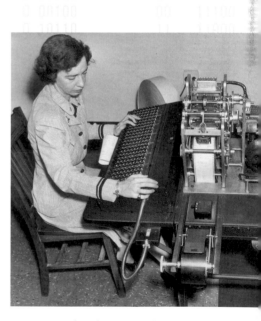

Grace Hopper's nickname was "Amazing Grace." The USS Hopper, a United States Navy guided missile destroyer, is named after her.

In Tulay 6-2 m 033 failed special speed test

1700   Started Cosine Tape (Sine check)
1525   Started Mult + Adder Test.
1545   Relay #70 Panel F
        (moth) in relay.

        First actual case of bug being found.
1700   closed down.

Left: *Ever been frustrated by a computer bug? Here's the first one ever. While Hopper and her crew were working on a computer in 1947, this moth got stuck in it and slowed it down. Hopper and her staff added this real computer bug to their log book. Below: Hopper and her staff in 1960 working at a UNIVAC I console. UNIVAC is short for Universal Automatic Computer.*

A compiler translates worded instructions into code that a computer can read. Hopper created COBOL, a computer programming language that uses entirely English words. COBOL (the name comes from the term "*common business-oriented language*") changed how people use computers.

Right: This reel of magnetic tape carried a complier for Hopper's invention COBOL. Below: Grace Hopper Celebration is the world's largest get-together of women who study computers or work with them! It's held every year with tech sessions, panels, workshops and a career fair.

AHA!

Nutty Putty

One of the side effects of World War II was a shortage of natural rubber. The government took steps to manage the problem, which included **rationing** rubber products and funding research into synthetic rubber.

Engineer James Wright created a rubbery material in 1943, but it was too soft to be a replacement. Instead of assuming that this new product—Wright called it Nutty Putty—was no good, he packed it into little plastic eggs and renamed it Silly Putty. Kids loved it—and they still do!

Astronauts took Silly Putty into space in 1968. They used it to hold their tools in place so they wouldn't float around in **microgravity**!

SEE YA!

Laser Cataract Treatment, 1986

Dr. Patricia Bath

(1942–)

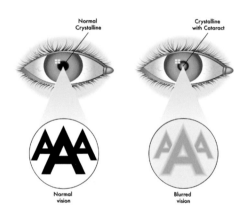

It's easy to see in this diagram how cataracts affect people's eyes.

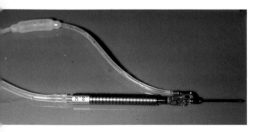

Patricia Bath's Laserphaco Probe is used around the world to treat cataracts.

W hen Patricia Bath was growing up in New York City in the mid-1940s, it was difficult for women and people of color to get into medical school, especially if they didn't have much money. But Bath worked hard, won a scholarship and graduated with a medical degree from Howard University in 1968.

In medical school, Bath became especially interested in helping patients with poor vision. Many suffered from cataracts, which cloud the lens in the eye and can make people's eyesight very bad. Treating cataracts involves removing the lens and replacing it with a synthetic transparent lens.

Bath always believed that she could improve cataract surgery. In 1981 she came up with the idea of a laser device to remove cataracts. However, her concept for laser cataract surgery was too advanced for existing technology.

Bath has continued to improve her invention. With the Laserphaco Probe, she's been able to give vision back to people who haven't been able to see for decades.

Finally in 1986 she was able to create the Laserphaco Probe, the laser device she had conceived of in 1981. Although it took years of research and testing, she finally received the patent for the Laserphaco Probe in 1988.

This invention began the era of laser cataract surgery. The goal of laser cataract surgery is to improve its precision, safety and efficacy to benefit patients.

Bath didn't stop there. She continued to invent and improve on her concept, which earned her several patents on cataract surgery.

AMAZING *and* TRUE

WHAT'S A PATENT?

Patricia Bath was the first African American woman to receive a patent for a medical purpose. A patent gives its owner the legal right to prevent others from making, using, selling and importing an invention.

Many people believe Alexander Graham Bell's patent for the telephone was the most valuable patent ever.

Some inventors, such as Alexander Fleming (page 36) and Marie Curie (page 25), chose not to patent their inventions. Although everyone can benefit from inventions, only the patent owners can make money from them.

CHAPTER NINE

BE OPEN TO POSSIBILITIES

Inventors have to see beyond what's right in front of them and be aware of other options. They may look at something ordinary in their lives and see how it can be used in a new way. Or if an experiment is giving an unexpected result, they may see nothing wrong with the surprising outcome.

While working with a vial of explosive nitroglycerin in 1866, Alfred Nobel accidentally dropped it. Yikes! He expected to be blown up! Instead, the Swedish chemist noticed, the sawdust on the floor absorbed the liquid. Nobel saw possibilities in this, which led to the creation of dynamite. (Nobel set up the well-known Nobel Prizes because he wanted to be famous for something more than inventing dynamite.)

AHA!

It's a Wonderful Toy

In 1943 American naval engineer Richard James was trying to create a spring to use with delicate equipment on ships. One day he accidentally knocked one of the springs he'd been working with off a shelf. James watched as it hit the floor and kept moving. Suddenly he saw the possibility of turning the spring into a toy.

James's wife, Betty, named the toy the Slinky. More than 300 million have been sold around the world. What a lot of slinking!

Being open to possibilities can lead to less explosive inventions too! New York tea and coffee seller Thomas Sullivan shipped out samples of tea to clients. He sent the loose leaves in little silk bags. Customers were supposed to remove the tea from the bag and put it in a pot. But users found it easier to leave the leaves in the bag. They even suggested Sullivan use a less finely woven fabric. So in 1904 Sullivan began selling tea bags made of gauze.

If something's bugging you, see what you can invent to fix it. You can research inventors online and find out about contests or meetings for inventors.

A GLOB OF GOO

Friction Matches, 1826

John Walker

(1781–1859)

John Walker made very little money from his invention, even though it really did change the world. Because he never applied for a patent, other people were able to produce and sell his matches, which were often carried in small metal canisters.

I've got to get that dried glob of goo off the end of my mixing stick, thought John Walker as he stirred a bubbling pot of chemicals. What happened next changed the world, but only because Walker was open to seeing possibilities.

Walker was a **pharmacist** in Stockton-on-Tees, England, in the early 1800s. He was fascinated by many scientific topics. One of his areas of interest was trying to invent safer, more effective explosives. He'd experimented with lots of chemicals in the little lab behind his store, but without success.

In 1826 Walker was using a stick to stir together two chemicals (antimony sulfide and potassium chlorate) with gum and starch. He was frustrated to see that part of the gooey mixture had hardened on the end of his stick. So Walker hurriedly scraped it on the floor of his lab to try to remove it. He was shocked when the end of the stick burst into flame!

Instead of ignoring this unexpected result, Walker was open to its possibilities. He made a number of 7.5 cm (3 in.) long matchsticks with the goo at the end. Then he amazed friends by pulling them between sheets of rough paper and setting them ablaze. The matches became known as friction matches because it was the friction between the match head and the paper that made the matches ignite.

Friction matches were easy for people to carry so they could quickly have fire wherever they wanted. Walker's invention changed how fire was created and used.

Walker received no popular recognition for inventing friction matches, so in 2015 British scientist Joe McGinnis recreated Walker's breakthrough invention, and artist Sarah Pickering (above) took photographs of the lit matches. Her photographs were then displayed in Stockton, where Walker lived.

ORIGINAL BABYSITTER UPDATED

Jolly Jumper, 1910

Susan Olivia Poole

(1889–1975)

Susan Olivia Poole had seven children. No wonder she was inspired to invent the Jolly Jumper!

When Susan Olivia Poole was growing up on the White Earth Indian Reservation in northwestern Minnesota, she noticed busy moms strapping their babies to cradle boards. While working out in the fields, the women would suspend the portable carriers from tree branches by leather straps. When the moms gave the branches a tug, the babies bounced and giggled happily. Rock-a-bye, baby!

In 1910 Poole's first baby was born. The busy mom remembered the cradle boards from her Ojibwa childhood, recognized the possibilities of this idea and decided to give it a modern twist. Using a cloth diaper as a sling seat, Poole hung the swing from a coiled spring attached to an ax handle. Her son loved the swing, and it kept him safe and happy, jumping and bouncing, while his mom worked.

Left: *When Poole started marketing the Jolly Jumper, babies and parents everywhere were thrilled.* Right: *One of Poole's grandchildren in an early Jolly Jumper.*

Poole made Jolly Jumpers for all seven of her children. Years later she made them for her grand-children as well. In 1948 Poole saw the possibility of selling her invention to other busy parents. Poole patented her invention in 1957, and babies are still jumping and bouncing in Jolly Jumpers today.

AMAZING *and* TRUE

INGENIOUS INDIGENOUS INVENTIONS

Indigenous people have invented many important things. For instance, they changed how people get around with inventions such as canoes (birchbark and dugout), moccasins, snowshoes and toboggans. The travois, a sled made of two poles harnessed to a dog or horse and including a platform or basket for carrying loads, is another Indigenous transportation invention.

In Canada's north, Inuit created the dogsled and kayak to make getting around easier. Inuit also invented the igloo and snow goggles—which evolved into sunglasses.

Duck decoys, megaphones for calling moose, tipis, pemmican (dried food made with shredded meat)—these are just a few other amazing Indigenous inventions.

IT STARTED WITH POTATOES

Television, 1927

Philo Farnsworth

(1906-1971)

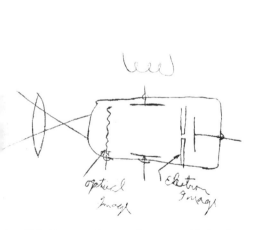

Philo Farnsworth was only 15 years old when he drew this sketch of how he thought an electronic TV camera could work.

Philo Farnsworth was an extraordinary teenage inventor and builder. At age thirteen he figured out how to use electricity to power the barn lights, sewing machine and washing machine on the farm that his family had moved to in Rigby, Idaho.

Farnsworth knew television had already been invented, but it was a mechanical television. That meant it used rotating disks with holes in them to scan, transmit and display pictures. The images were small and fuzzy.

Scientists were looking for a way to improve TV. They'd experimented with tubes that use a focused beam of electrons—very small particles with a negative electrical charge—to display images (they're called cathode ray tubes). But so far they hadn't had any luck with electronic television.

Farnsworth had many chores on his family's farm, including plowing the potato field. One day he stopped to look at the side-by-side, straight rows of dirt stretching across the field. He got the idea of breaking down an image into **parallel lines** of light that could be transmitted as electrons to a screen somewhere else. When the electrons were changed back into lines of light, the original picture appeared on the screen.

By being open to possibilities, Farnsworth figured out the basic idea behind electronic television. He kept working on the concept. In 1927, when Farnsworth was just twenty-one, he transmitted the first electronic television image from one room to another by scanning a photo in a series of parallel lines.

Farnsworth thought people would use television to learn and to find out more about the world. He felt people instead were wasting their time watching silly shows. Farnsworth was so disappointed with his invention that he never allowed a TV in his own home!

Farnsworth is on the left in this photo of a scene being filmed for television.

electronic

Feeding Device

DECODING
IN THE WAR

discovering
Fossils

Fig. 7

2,292,387

SECRET COMMUNICATION SYSTEM

Hedy Kiesler Markey, Los Angeles, and George Antheil, Manhattan Beach, Calif.

Application June 10, 1941, Serial No. 397,412

6 Claims. (Cl. 250—2)

This invention relates broadly to secret communication systems involving the use of carrier waves of different frequencies, and is especially useful in the remote control of dirigible craft, such as torpedoes.

An object of the invention is to provide a method of secret communication which is relatively simple and reliable in operation, but at the same time is difficult to discover or decipher.

CHAPTER TEN
BELIEVE IN YOURSELF

Failure can be the best teacher and can help an inventor or scientist discover the path to success. Despite failing, innovators trust their feelings and instincts. They never take no for an answer when a new idea is rejected or misunderstood. They persist until someone is willing to take a chance on their new idea.

But believing in yourself and your work isn't easy.

When Toronto-born Joe Shuster moved to Cleveland, he befriended Jerry Siegel at school. Shuster loved to draw and Siegel loved to write, and while they were in high school they invented a superhero they were sure would be perfect for comic books. They called their superhero Superman, but when they tried to get someone interested in publishing comics about their "man of steel," all they heard was a loud *no*. But they didn't take no for an answer. It took almost six years and some changes before someone recognized that Superman had real potential. In June 1938 Superman hit the comic-book shelves. He was a huge success, and to this day readers and moviegoers of all ages are riveted to his perilous adventures.

Imagine how amazed Shuster and Siegel would be if they knew that a copy of their first Superman comic from 1938 sold at auction in 2016 for nearly a million dollars!

> **"Don't let others discourage you or tell you that you can't do it. In my day, I was told women didn't go into chemistry. I saw no reason why we couldn't."**
>
> —Gertrude B. Elion, scientist

LOOK WHAT I FOUND

Discovering Fossils, 1811

Mary Anning
(1799–1847)

Mary Anning found the fossils of a plesiosaur like this one on the fossil-rich Jurassic Coast of Dorset, England. You can hunt for fossils there today. Just be careful you don't fall off the cliffs.

Mary Anning had a good eye and a sharp mind. She was born in 1799 to a poor family in Lyme Regis, England. It was an area rich in **fossils**—the remains of ancient organisms or creatures such as dinosaurs. Scientists and collectors were fascinated by fossils, and Anning was skilled at recognizing and finding them in the coastal cliffs near her home. The cliffs could be dangerous, especially in winter—the storms that battered them often created landslides. Despite the danger, Anning frequently ventured there in winter, because the slides exposed new fossils.

She discovered her first significant fossils when she was about twelve. By 1820 she had taken charge of the family fossil-collecting business. One of her most important finds was the first plesiosaur

The beautiful Jurassic Coast of England still attracts fossil hunters who hope to find fossils like the ones pictured below. It has been designated a World Heritage Site.

Anning wrote and signed this letter about her exciting discovery of a plesiosaur on the Jurassic Coast.

Scale One Inch to each Foot

Sir,

I have endeavoured by a rough sketch to give you some idea of what it is like, for you understood me right in thinking that I said it was the supposed plesiosaurus, but its remarkable long neck and small head, shows that it does not in the least agree with their conjectures; in its analogy to the Ichthyosaurus, it is large and heavy, but one thing I may venture to assure you it is the first and only one discovered in Europe, Colonel Birch offered one hundred guineas for it unseen, but your letter came one days post before but

(a kind of dinosaur). Anning made drawings, fixed fossils on cement and made them available to museums, collectors and scientists.

Many scientists of her day couldn't believe that a young woman with so little education could become a fossil expert. Yet even those who were skeptical were impressed with her diligence, intelligence and observational skills, and they visited Anning to discuss her ideas and discoveries. In 1826 Anning had saved enough money to open a shop called Anning's Fossil Depot, where she sold fossils directly.

After she died, the famous author Charles Dickens wrote: "The carpenter's daughter has won a name for herself, and has deserved to win it."

If you want to learn more about natural history, head to the Natural History Museum in London and explore its fascinating displays about life on Earth.

AMAZING *and* TRUE

MARY'S AMAZING SHELLS

Some people claim that Mary Anning inspired the famous tongue twister "she sells sea shells by the seashore."

STAR INVENTOR

Decoding in the War, 1942

Hedy Lamarr

(1914–2000)

Beautiful actress Hedy Lamarr might have played a supporting role in this movie, but in real life she was an important inventor.

Hedy Lamarr was more than a glamorous Hollywood actress. She was also an inventor who worked on radio signals to help defeat the Nazis in World War II. Lamarr's varied career started in Austria when she (then known as Hedwig Eva Maria Kiesler) married an older, very rich Austrian munitions (weapons and ammunition) manufacturer and dealer who hung around with Fascist leaders, like Mussolini, and the scientists working for them.

She lived in a castle, but living in a castle with an abusive husband was no fairy tale. One day she managed to escape the marriage, and eventually she reached the United States. That's where she began her acting career and changed her name to Hedy Lamarr. And that's where Lamarr began inventing. Her early inventions included an improved traffic stoplight, an aid to help people with

Hedy Lamarr was a star actress, inventor and thinker!

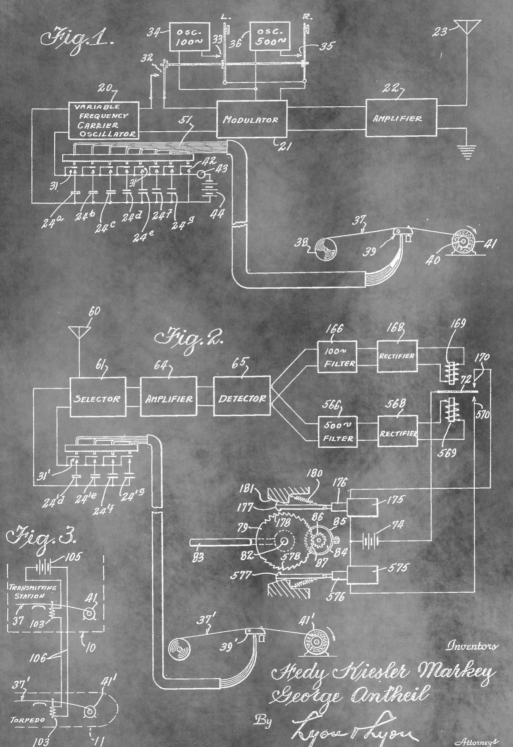

Inventors

Hedy Kiesler Markey
George Antheil

By *Lyon & Lyon*

Attorneys

limited mobility get in and out of the bath, a fluorescent dog collar and a quick way to create carbonated drinks. During World War II Lamarr teamed with composer George Antheil to invent radio signals that would help jam torpedoes and stop them from damaging Allied ships.

Unfortunately, it took the Navy years to use their invention effectively, but finally, in 1962, an updated version was employed on Navy ships. Lamarr and Antheil's system was an early form of wireless communication technology.

Acting paid Lamarr's bills, but her passion was inventing.

Left: *Lamarr's secret communication system was designed to help the Allies defend their citizens in World War II.*

AMAZING *and* TRUE

SURPRISING HEDY

Many of Hedy Lamarr's acting roles bored her. She took up inventing not just because she was creative but also because she loved a challenge. She said, "All creative people want to do the unexpected."

TRY THIS

Electronic Feeding Device, 1951

Bessie Blount Griffin

(1914–2009)

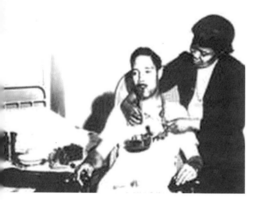

Bessie Blount Griffin cared deeply about helping people, and that desire drove her to invent tools to aid patients. In 1951 she received a patent for a portable receptacle support. Despite all her efforts, Griffin's inventions were unappreciated in her own country.

Becoming a physical therapist as a black woman in Chicago before World War II wasn't easy, but Bessie Blount Griffin was determined. As a physical therapist working with injured soldiers, she saw how difficult and frustrating it was for **amputees** to manage daily activities, and she wanted to help. After analyzing the problem, Griffin invented a machine to help amputees feed themselves. She believed this was an important way to help them feel more independent. The tube she designed allowed patients to control how much food they ate and how quickly they ate it. Later she invented a simple device that allowed patients to balance a bowl, cup or dish. Griffin received a patent for that invention in 1951.

Griffin tried selling her idea to veterans' associations. but they weren't interested. She even appeared on

Griffin (right) appeared on radio and TV to talk about her work and inventions.

a TV show called *The Big Idea*, hoping publicity would encourage the American government to use her invention. That didn't work either. What now? Try the French! So Griffin donated her invention to France, where it was used extensively with patients.

Griffin's friend Theodore M. Edison, son of the famous inventor Thomas Edison, believed in her, and they discussed ways to innovate and create new products. When Griffin invented a disposable cardboard basin for patients, she again found no interest in the US. This time she sold the idea to a company in Belgium, and the basin was used in their hospitals.

> "It's not that I'm so smart, it's just that I stay with problems longer."
>
> —Albert Einstein, scientist

CHAPTER ELEVEN
ACCIDENTAL GENIUSES—A NEW GENERATION

More and more young people are inventing things. Modern technology makes it easy to find out what inventions are needed, obtain help from other inventors and promote new innovations.

Teenager Anurudh Ganesan was heartbroken to learn that 1.5 million kids died in 2008 from diseases that are preventable with a **vaccine**. A vaccine is a solution that helps keep a person from getting a disease, but it has to be kept chilled or it won't be effective. Ganesan believed in himself and felt he could do something to help keep vaccines cool. He invented a wheel-powered refrigeration system that uses no ice or electricity and can be hitched to a bicycle or pulled by a person or an animal. Ganesan's invention, called the VAXXWAGON, could save millions of lives.

When Ann (Andini) Makosinski was in high school, she invented the Hollow Flashlight, which is powered by the heat of the hand. No wonder the student from Victoria, British Columbia, was named one of *Time* magazine's *30 Under 30* in 2014. Makosinski is tweaking her device to make it more efficient, and she's also open to working on other inventions, including a mug that uses the heat from the hot drink it's holding to charge a cell phone.

AHA!

Robotic Worms

Paying attention in science class and learning about earthworms led David Cohen of Dallas, Texas, to build and write the code for a robotic "earthworm" that can squeeze into places too tiny or dangerous for people or rescue dogs to go. Loaded with heat-sensing technology and lifesaving programs, Cohen's worm can locate and rescue people trapped in buildings after an earthquake or fire.

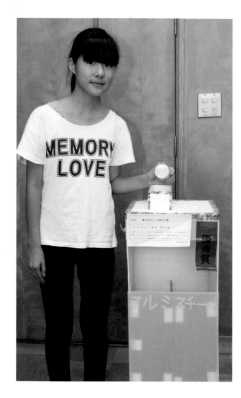

MAGNET MAGIC

Self-Separating Recycling Bin, 2014

Asuka Kamiya

(2003–)

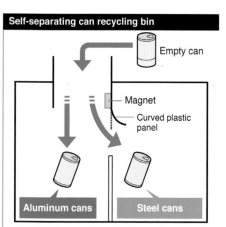

Self-separating can recycling bin

Empty can

Magnet

Curved plastic panel

Aluminum cans

Steel cans

CHUNICHI SHIMBUN GRAPHIC

The idea behind Asuka Kamiya's invention is simple, but it took an accidental genius to think of it.

Over the summer in fifth grade, Asuka Kamiya from the Aichi Prefecture in Japan had to complete a science project. She decided to build an invention that would help her grandfather, a grocery-store owner. She had watched him struggle to separate different types of cans for recycling and thought there must be a better way.

Kamiya remembered an experiment her class had done in third grade that used magnets, aluminum plates and steel plates. The experiment showed that steel is attracted to magnets but aluminum isn't. Kamiya thought she could use this fact to create a self-separating recycling bin and make her grandfather's life easier.

It took a lot of experimenting, but eventually Kamiya came up with a bin design that worked well. A magnet at the top of the bin makes the aluminum cans fall one way and the steel cans drop in a different direction.

Now Kamiya is one of the few elementary-school students in Japan to hold a patent. She advises other young inventors not to be afraid to try. "Try your ideas even if they don't work," encourages Kamiya. "Even if something doesn't work, you may discover something new. Just try it anyway. You'll find a way, if you try!"

You can watch Asuka demonstrating her invention. Go to youtube.com/ watch?v=onNCXFT_Ots&t=14s to check out a video.

AHA!

Glowing Jellyfish Windows

Nikita Rafikov from Evans, Georgia, found out about jellyfish and used his knowledge to invent an amazing way to make homes brighter. In 2014, when he was 11, he developed a way to embed green fluorescent protein (GFP) from jellyfish into windows. GFP is what creates **bioluminescence** (light produced by living organisms) in jellyfish. Thanks to Rafikov, it also creates efficient glass that lights homes without using electricity.

ALGAE MOBILE

EcoTube, 2008

Param Jaggi
(1994–)

When Param Jaggi realized that car exhaust was contributing to climate change, he decided to do something to help save the planet.

When Param Jaggi was a little boy, he liked to break things to figure out what was inside them. He started with his toys, but when he was five and he broke a computer, his parents were rather upset!

Today Jaggi still likes to break things to look inside them, but he likes to build things too. This amazing inventor was born in Mumbai, India, but grew up in Plano, Texas. He began inventing when he was twelve years old and applied for his first patent a year later. He's fascinated by carbon dioxide, a gas that occurs naturally in Earth's atmosphere. But the amount of this gas has been greatly increased by car exhaust. That's a problem, because it's led to global warming.

Algae, the green substance you can see on the water here, make most of Earth's oxygen. Some algae look like plants, but they're not plants or animals. Many live in oceans and marshes, but they also live in soil and on leaves, as well as on turtles and even polar bears!

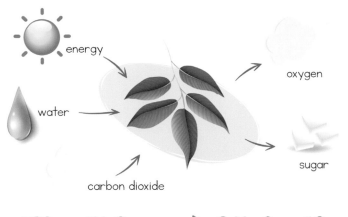

$$6CO_2 + 6H_2O \longrightarrow C_6H_{12}O_6 + 6O_2$$

Plants depend on photosynthesis to change light energy, such as sunlight, into chemical energy. A plant can store this chemical energy and use it later for fuel to help it grow.

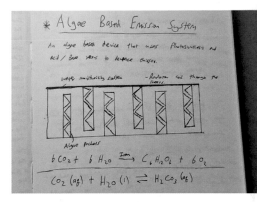

Here's the EcoTube design that Jaggi first created when he was thirteen. His invention evolved a lot!

Jaggi wanted to help the environment, so he connected that desire with his knowledge about carbon dioxide and invented the EcoTube. The EcoTube works by passing a car's exhaust fumes through live algae. That makes **photosynthesis** take place, which is the process through which plants absorb sunshine (light), water and carbon dioxide to create sugars they can use as food. Plants release oxygen, which people need to breathe, during the process.

So the EcoTube changes carbon dioxide in a car's exhaust into oxygen and sugar, and that's a lot better for the environment. Jaggi's device can be fitted to a car's tailpipe to reduce carbon emissions by up to 50 percent. He has lots of other ideas for inventions to help the environment and wants to encourage other young people to invent and innovate.

The EcoTube fits directly onto the exhaust pipe of any car. It uses basic biological and chemical processes to reduce the car's carbon dioxide emissions.

CLEAN UP THAT OILY GOOP

Tailings Filter, 2014

Hayley Todesco

(1996–)

This photo shows tailings pouring into a tailings pond. The toxic compounds are stored in these large basins to allow them to break down. Hayley Todesco aims to make that process faster with her invention.

Hayley Todesco was in fifth grade in Calgary, Alberta, when she first saw the device that would later inspire her invention. In her classroom she watched as muddy water was poured through a sand filter and emerged clean at the bottom.

Years later, when Todesco was looking for a science-fair project idea, she remembered that filter. Growing up in Alberta, Todesco knew about **tailings**—the toxic waste that remains after oil is extracted from oil sands, which are a mixture of sand, water, clay and oil (bitumen). She was also interested in **bioreactors**, which are devices that use bacteria to break down waste. So Todesco decided to use bacteria to build filters that could break down the tailings.

Oil sands tailings ponds inspired Todesco's invention, like this one located north of Fort McMurray, Alberta.

Todesco won the 2014 Stockholm Junior Water Prize for her work using filters on contaminated water in tailings ponds. She won $15,000, and her school won $5,000.

AMAZING *and* TRUE

INVENTIVE INSPIRATION

It's easy to find out more about these young inventors. Check out their websites or follow them on Facebook, Instagram or Twitter. You'll discover what inspires these innovators and the obstacles they've overcome. They have a lot to say about what it's like to be a young inventor and how to make sure your invention is taken seriously by adults.

Most of the items Todesco needed to build her filters she picked up at hardware and dollar stores. The bacteria were given to her by a local university. It took Todesco two years to perfect her invention—she took her time to make sure it was just right.

Todesco says her filters can break down the toxic compounds in tailings fourteen times faster than if they just sit in tailings ponds, which is the current method of dealing with them. In 2014 her invention won the worldwide Google Science Fair prize in the category for seventeen- to eighteen-year-olds.

Are you feeling inspired by these stories of other kids today who are inventors? Then get inventing! There are lots of ways you can be an accidental genius too.

So you want to be an accidental genius?

1. **DON'T BE AFRAID TO TRY:** If one experiment doesn't work, try another until you've exhausted all possibilities. Then try again.

2. **GET KNOWLEDGE AND USE IT:** Observe. Listen. Consult others. Read everything on the subject that you can. Always be open to new ideas and directions.

3. **PAY ATTENTION:** Be curious and ask lots of questions. Pay special attention when your work gives you a surprising result.

4. **MAKE CONNECTIONS:** Analyze what's already been done and stay alert and open to new possibilities.

5. **IT TAKES TIME:** Keep working, assessing your results and looking for the next step, no matter how long it takes.

6. **BE PERSISTENT:** Never take no for an answer and never give up, even if it takes many tries to complete your invention.

7. **FAILURE IS PART OF THE PROCESS:** See failures and accidents as opportunities. Keep experimenting and inventing despite your failures.

8. **DON'T MAKE ASSUMPTIONS:** No matter how tough it is to gather the data or how much time it takes, only use information you know is correct or can check.

9. **BE OPEN TO POSSIBILITIES:** Look beyond what's right in front of you and be aware of other options.

10. **BELIEVE IN YOURSELF:** Trust your feelings and instincts and remember that luck and timing are part of the process.

GLOSSARY

adhesive—a substance that bonds objects or materials together

amputee—a person who has had part of an arm or leg cut off

antibiotic—a substance that kills or slows the growth of disease-causing microscopic organisms

bacteria—tiny, single-celled organisms that live in soil and water or the bodies of plants and animals

bioluminescence—light produced by living organisms

bioreactors—devices that use bacteria to break down waste

cathode ray—a flow of electrons, one of the three tiny particles that make up an atom, from a closed container that contains no air

classify—to arrange something in a group or as part of a category

corrode—to gradually destroy or "eat away"

cosmonaut—an astronaut from the Soviet space program

counterweight—a weight that balances other weights by exerting an opposite force

data—facts and information collected to use in a discussion or calculation

displacing—removing or replacing

electric current—a flow of electric charge through a wire or circuit

entrepreneur—person who organizes, manages and assumes the risks of a business

etching—making designs on a hard material by "eating" lines into the material's surface

fossil—the remains or impression of a plant or animal from a past era that has been preserved in the Earth's crust

herpes—a group of viral diseases that affect the skin or nervous system

hinge—a movable part that allows something to open, close or swing

kerosene—a light fuel used in heaters and lamps

leukemia—a cancer in which there is an abnormal increase in white blood cells, which crowd out red blood cells

mass-produce—to produce or manufacture in large quantities

metallurgy—the scientific study of the properties and uses of metals

microgravity—the condition in which the pull of gravity is very weak; often called zero gravity or weightlessness

mold—a fungus that grows in the form of tiny, threadlike structures and often appears fuzzy or furry

molecule—an electrically neutral group of two or more atoms, held together by chemical bonds

nitric acid—a corrosive colorless or yellowish liquid used in the making of dyes, explosives and fertilizers

nutrient—a substance that plants and animals use to survive and grow

obsolete—outdated or no longer being produced

oncologist—a doctor who diagnoses and treats cancer

organism—any individual living thing that can function on its own, whether animal, plant or single-celled life form

parallel lines—lines that run in the same direction and at the same distance apart

patent—an official document that gives an inventor the right to make, sell or use an invention

pharmacist—a health-care professional who prepares and sells medicinal drugs

photosynthesis—the process through which plants absorb light, water and carbon dioxide to create food and release oxygen

radar—a system for detecting the presence, speed and direction of an object, such as an aircraft or ship, using radio waves

radiation—energy in the form of light, sound or heat that moves from one place to another

rationing—controlling how scarce items are used or distributed

silicon—a gray chemical element found in rocks and sand and used to make computers and other electronics

stainless steel—a mixture of steel and chromium that doesn't easily corrode, rust or stain

synthetic—artificial or manufactured

tailings—the residue left over from mining and extracting resources

tenacity—the quality of being determined and never giving up

vaccine—a solution that helps keep a person from getting a disease

variable stars—stars whose brightness changes regularly or irregularly

wireless communication—the transfer of information or power using radio signals

RESOURCES

PRINT

Altman, Linda Jacobs. *Women Inventors*. New York, NY: Facts on File, 1997.

Blashfield, Jean F. *Women Inventors*. Mankato, MN: Capstone Press Inc., 1996.

Braun, Sandra. *Incredible Women Inventors*. Toronto, ON: Second Story Press, 2006.

Challoner, Jack. *1001 Inventions that Changed the World*. Hauppauge, NY: Barron's Educational Series, 2009.

Jaffé, Deborah. *Ingenious Women: From Tincture of Saffron to Flying Machines*. Stroud, UK: The History Press, 2004.

Johnston, David, and Tom Jenkins. *Ingenious: How Canadian Innovators Made the World Smaller, Smarter, Kinder, Safer, Healthier, Wealthier and Happier*. Toronto, ON: McClelland & Stewart, 2017.

———. *Innovation Nation: How Canadian Innovators Made the World Smarter, Smaller, Kinder, Safer, Healthier, Wealthier, Happier*. Toronto, ON: Tundra Books, 2017.

Jones, Charlotte Foltz. *Mistakes that Worked*. New York, NY: Random House Children's Books, 2016.

Kulling, Monica. *In the Bag!: Margaret Knight Wraps It Up*. Toronto, ON: Tundra Books, 2013.

Maggs, Sam. *Wonder Women: 25 Innovators, Inventors, and Trailblazers Who Changed History*. Philadelphia, PA: Quirk Books, 2016.

Morgan, George D. *Rocket Girl: The Story of Mary Sherman Morgan, America's First Female Rocket Scientist*. Amherst, NY: Prometheus Books, 2013.

Swaby, Rachel. *Trailblazers: 33 Women in Science Who Changed the World*. New York, NY: Random House Children's Books, 2016.

Thimmesh, Catherine, and Melissa Sweet. *Girls Think of Everything: Stories of Ingenious Inventions by Women*. Boston, MA: HMH Books for Young Readers, 2002.

Vare, Ethlie Ann. *Women Inventors and Their Discoveries*. Minneapolis, MN: Oliver Press Inc., 1993.

Verstraete, Larry. *Whose Bright Idea Was It?* Richmond Hill, ON: Scholastic Canada, 1997.

Weiner, Eric. *The Geography of Genius*. New York, NY: Simon & Schuster, 2016.

Wood, Annie. *Canadian Women Invent*. Toronto, ON: Inventive Women Inc., 2001.

Wyatt, Valerie. *Inventions*. Toronto, ON: Kids Can Press, 2003.

———. *Everything You Wanted to Know About Inventions*. Toronto, ON: Owl Books, 1987.

FILM

Dean, Alexandra. *Bombshell: The Hedy Lamarr Story*. New York, NY: Reframed Pictures, 2017.

ONLINE

Anurudh Ganesan: solve.mit.edu/users/anurudh-ganesan

Asuka Kamiya: www.youtube.com/watch?v=0nNCXFT_Ots

Encyclopedia of World Biography: encyclopedia.com

Extreme Tech: extremetech.com

Famous Scientists: The Art of Genius: famousscientists.org

Famous Women Inventors: women-inventors.com

Historical Inventors: lemelson.mit.edu/resources

InventHelp: inventhelp.com/links/inventing-for-kids-parents-and-teachers

Inventive Kids: inventivekids.com

Jolly Jumper: 216.95.206.43/history

Louis Braille: www.afb.org/LouisBrailleMuseum/

Mandy Haberman: mandyhaberman.com/

National Inventors Hall of Fame: invent.org

Nobel Prize: nobelprize.org

Param Jaggi: paramjaggi.com/

Razor Scooter: razor.com/

Science History Institute: sciencehistory.org/

Slinky: alexbrands.com/pa_brand/slinky/

WD-40: wd40.com/

INDEX

Page numbers in **bold** indicate an image; there may also be text related to the same topic on that page.

PHOTO CREDITS

CHAPTER ONE: Dr. Leo Hendrik Baekeland: p. 10 New York Public Library/Science Source; p. 11 (top) courtesy of the Science History Institute, (right) National Museum of American History, Gift of Union Carbide Corporation, Specialty Chemicals Division; p. 12 (bottom) Linda Williams/Dreamstime.com; p. 13 courtesy of Brodie Hemmings-Sykes. **Stephanie Kwolek**: p. 14 (top and left) and p. 15 Hagley Museum and Library; p. 16 (top) PongMoji/Shutterstock.com, (left) Dmitri Mihhailov/Dreamstime.com; p. 17 gorillaimages/Shutterstock.com. **Jamie Link:** p. 18 (top) courtesy of Jamie Link, (left) UC San Diego, Jacobs School of Engineering; p. 19 (top) courtesy of Jamie Link.

CHAPTER TWO: Williamina Paton Stevens Fleming: p. 22 Williamina Paton Stevens Fleming (1857–1911), circa 1890s, Courtesy Curator of Astronomical Photographs at Harvard College Observatory; p. 23 (top) Observatory [analysis of stellar spectra], 1891, HUV 1210 (9-6), olvwork289693, Harvard University Archives, and (right) NASA/ESA/Hubble Heritage Team. **Dr. Wilhelm Röntgen:** p. 24 (top and left) Wikipedia commons; p. 25 Fer Gregory/Shutterstock.com. **Dr. Wilfred G. Bigelow and Dr. John C. Callaghan:** p. 26 (top and left) and p. 27 (top) courtesy of the National Research Council.

CHAPTER THREE: Mary Anderson: p. 30 (top and left) Wikipedia commons, p. 31 Google patents, US Patent 743801. **George Washington Carver:** p. 32 (top) Frances Benjamin Johnston Collection, Library of Congress, (left) Tuskegee Institute National Historic Site, National Parks Service; p. 33 (top) USDA History Collection, Special Collections, National Agricultural Library; p. 34 (left) Tuskegee Institute National Historic Site, National Parks Service, (bottom) Scott Bauer/courtesy of USDA Natural Resources Conservation Service; p. 35 (top) U.S. Department of Agriculture, (right) courtesy of the George Washington Carver Science Fair, (bottom) Prillfoto/Dreamstime.com. **Sir Alexander Fleming:** p. 36 (top) Wikipedia commons, (left) Everett Historical/Shutterstock.com; p. 37 (top) science photo/Shutterstockcom.

CHAPTER FOUR: Sarah E. Goode: p. 41 courtesy of Reggie Smith, Smith-Lenoir Graphic Creations; p. 42 courtesy of Darryl Adrian/Murphy Wall-Bed Victoria; p. 43 (right) Google Patents, US Patent 322177A, (bottom) courtesy of dbHMS. **George de Mestral:** p. 44 (top) Charles de Mestral, (left) Google Patents, US Patent 3009235A; p. 45 Josep Curto/Dreamstime.com. **Percy Spencer:** p. 46 (top) courtesy of Raytheon Company, (left) Wikipedia commons; p. 47 (bottom) Neil Trafford.

CHAPTER FIVE: Frank Epperson: p. 50 (top) Bettmann/Getty Images; p. 51 (bottom) cali9/iStockphoto.com. **Dr. Vera Peters:** p. 52 (top) courtesy of Charles Hayter, (left) courtesy of Dr. Jennifer Ingram; p. 53 photo by Bruce Peters and courtesy of the Alumnae Theatre. **Dr. Spencer Silver and Art Fry:** p. 54 Ewapix/Dreamstime.com; p. 55 (top) courtesy of National Inventors Hall of Fame, (right) Kenishirotie/Dreamstime.com; p. 56 courtesy of National Inventors Hall of Fame; p. 57 (top) courtesy of Ben Brucker.

CHAPTER SIX: George Nissen: p. 60 (top and left) Wikipedia commons; p. 61 (top) Tim Blake, Nissen Trampoline Company, (right) Hrecheniuk Oleksii/Dreamstime.com. **Dr. Narinder Singh Kapany:** p. 63 courtesy of The Sikh Foundation; p. 63 (top) Satjiv Chahal, courtesy of The Sikh Foundation, (right) Gualtiero Boffi/Shutterstock.com; p. 64 Nikkytok/Dreamstime.com; p. 65 (bottom) Poungsaed-Studio/Shutterstock.com. **Mary Sherman Morgan:** p. 66 (top) George Morgan/Wikipedia commons, (left) Smithsonian Air and Space Museum; p. 67 (top) Wikipedia commons.

CHAPTER SEVEN: Margaret Knight: p. 71 (bottom) Division of Culture and the Arts, National Museum of American History, Smithsonian Institution. **Dr. John Harvey Kellogg and Will Keith "W.K." Kellogg:** p. 72 Bentley Image Bank, Bentley Historical Library; p. 73 (top) George Grantham Bain Collection, Library of Congress, (right) Wikipedia commons; p. 74 (top) Bain News Service, Library of Congress; p. 75 Ejwhite/Dreamstime.com. **Gino Tsai:** p. 77 Glenn Beltz/Flickr.

CHAPTER EIGHT: Dr. Roy Plunkett: p. 80 (top) courtesy of the Pleasant Hill History Center, (left) Wikipedia commons; p. 81 (top) Hagley Museum and Library, (right) Minko Dima/Shutterstock.com. **Dr. Grace Hopper:** p. 82 and 83 (top) courtesy of Unisys and Hagley Museum and Library, (right) New York Public Library/Science Source; p. 84 courtesy of Unisys and Hagley Museum and Library, (inset) Courtesy of the Naval Surface Warfare Center; p. 85 (center) Division of Culture and the Arts, National Museum of American History, Smithsonian Institution, (bottom) Grace Hopper Celebration, AnitaB.org. **Dr. Patricia Bath:** p. 86 (top and bottom left) © copyright owner Dr. Patricia Bath, (left) Rob3000/Dreamstime.com; p. 87 (top) © copyright owner Dr. Patricia Bath.

CHAPTER NINE: John Walker: p. 90 (top and left) Science and Society Museum; p. 91 courtesy of Stuart Boulton. **Susan Olivia Poole:** p. 92 and 93 (all) courtesy of Julie Shepherd and the family of Susan Olivia Poole. **Philo Farnsworth:** p. 94 (top) Engineering and Technology History Wiki/Creative Commons, (left) public domain; p. 95 Engineering and Technology History Wiki/Creative Commons.

CHAPTER TEN: Mary Anning: p. 98 (top) Wikipedia commons, (left) public domain; p. 99 (top) Patrick Wang/Dreamstime.com, (bottom) Chris Andrew/Flickr; p. 100 Wikipedia commons; p. 101 (top) Slawek Kozakiewicz/Dreamstime.com. **Hedy Lamarr:** p. 102 (top and left) and p. 103 Wikipedia commons; p. 104 Google Patents, US Patent 2292387; p. 105 (top) Wikipedia commons. **Bessie Blount Griffin:** p. 106 (top and left) public domain; p. 107 image from *The Crisis*, Aug-Sep 1965 issue, Google Books.

CHAPTER ELEVEN: p. 108 Ann Makosinski photo courtesy of Rick Collins. **Asuka Kamiya:** p. 110 (top and left) Chunichi Shimbun; p. 111 screen capture of TedxKyoto. **Param Jaggi:** p. 112 and p. 113 (top) courtesy of Param Jaggi, (right) Felix Mizioznikov/Dreamstime.com; p. 114 CasarsaGuru/Shutterstock.com; p. 115 (top) Blueringmedia/Dreamstime.com, (right and bottom right) courtesy of Param Jaggi. **Hayley Todesco:** p. 116 (top) Kesia Dias/courtesy of *The Gateway*, (right) Francis Black/iStockphoto.com; p. 117 Donny Ash/Shutterstock.com; p. 118 courtesy of Stockholm International Water Institute, SIWI.

Every effort has been made to locate and credit the correct copyright owners of the images used in this book. The publisher apologizes for any errors or omissions and would be grateful if notified of corrections that should be made in future reprints or editions.

ACKNOWLEDGMENTS

Many thanks to Sarah Harvey for her fine editing skills and for helping to make writing this book a pleasure. Big thanks as well to designer Teresa Bubela, illustrator Jenn Playford and copy editor Vivian Sinclair for their talents and insights.

Liz says: Many thanks to Frieda, my genius co-writer—it's always wonderful to work on another book with her. Thanks also to Frank Anderson for his assistance with research and his helpful suggestions. Special thanks to Paul for his help and for being my favorite genius!

I've always been interested in science and inventing. I dedicated this book to my friend Michele because we used to work together to enter science fairs. I still remember one project we did called "How Do Birds Fly?"

To show how a bird's wings move as they propel the bird through the air, we created a zoetrope. It's an animation device that consists of a sequence of drawings or photographs placed in a drum. When a viewer looks through a hole at the images and spins the drum, she gets the sense that she's seeing movement.

Michele drew the pictures of a bird's wings flapping—she's a really good artist—and we put the pictures together in sequence in a round drum. Then we built a box with a small hole in it for people to look through, and added a crank so they could turn the drum and see the bird "fly."

People loved the zoetrope, and they learned a lot about flight. And Michele and I learned how greasy people's foreheads are! Every time people leaned against the box to look in at the images, they left an oily mark. We were lucky enough to win at our first science fair, so before we headed to the next one, we glued a circle of vinyl around the peephole. The vinyl made the box look better, and we could easily clean it.

That was just one of the science-fair projects Michele and I took part in. Science is amazing, surprising and fun. Inventing is a great way to use your passion for science to solve problems. Give it a try!

Frieda says: It was a joy discovering each individual's story and accomplishments in *How to Become an Accidental Genius*. It was fascinating learning about so many unsung women and men whose work changed our lives. Researching their lives made me realize how important it is to be persistent and resilient and never take no for an answer.

I loved working with my gifted co-author, Elizabeth MacLeod. We've written four books together (so far), and Liz is the perfect collaborator. She's also fun to work with and generous in sharing her knowledge, ideas and her amazing chocolate-chip cookies.

Some of the innovators we profile in *Accidental Genius* were also lucky to have terrific collaborators (although I don't think anyone had a collaborator who made cookies as good as Liz's). But even those innovators who worked alone knew that their discoveries were built on the work of others before them. Each innovator studied, analyzed and experimented to create something new. When they failed, they tried again and again till they finally succeeded.

I'm grateful to the authors of the many articles and books about the people profiled in our book. Their work helped shape *Accidental Genius*.

Thanks also to my husband, Bill, for his support and smart suggestions.

ABOUT THE AUTHORS

Biographies, picture books, cookbooks—**Elizabeth MacLeod** has written them all and more. She has won many awards for her writing, including the Norma Fleck Award for Canadian Children's Non-Fiction, as well as Children's Choice awards across Canada. Liz is very curious and loves discovering incredible facts and sharing them with readers. With a university degree in biology, Liz has a special interest in science and inventors. For this book, Liz especially enjoyed writing about incredible female inventors such as Mary Anderson and Mary Sherman Morgan.

Frieda Wishinsky is the international award-winning author of over seventy books. She writes picture books, chapter books, novels and nonfiction. Her books have been translated into many languages, and her picture book *Please, Louise!* won the 2008 Marilyn Baillie Picture Book Award. She is also the author of the popular *Canadian Flyer Adventures* and *Survival* series. Frieda loves humor, travel, gardens, chocolate and sharing the writing process. For more information, visit friedawishinsky.com.